Extreme Walking

Extreme Walking

Extrabiblical Books and the Bible

Tom de Bruin

CASCADE *Books* • Eugene, Oregon

EXTREME WALKING
Extrabiblical Books and the Bible

Copyright © 2018 Tom de Bruin. All rights reserved. Except for brief quotations in critical publications or reviews, no part of this book may be reproduced in any manner without prior written permission from the publisher. Write: Permissions, Wipf and Stock Publishers, 199 W. 8th Ave., Suite 3, Eugene, OR 97401.

Cascade Books
An Imprint of Wipf and Stock Publishers
199 W. 8th Ave., Suite 3
Eugene, OR 97401

www.wipfandstock.com

PAPERBACK ISBN: 978-1-5326-1575-7
HARDCOVER ISBN: 978-1-5326-1577-1
EBOOK ISBN: 978-1-5326-1576-4

Cataloguing-in-Publication data:

Names: De Bruin, Tom.
Title: Extreme walking : extrabiblical books and the Bible / Tom de Bruin.
Description: Eugene, OR: Cascade Books, 2018 | Includes bibliographical references.
Identifiers: ISBN 978-1-5326-1575-7 (paperback) | ISBN 978-1-5326-1577-1 (hardcover) | ISBN 978-1-5326-1576-4 (ebook)
Subjects: LCSH: Apocryphal books Old Testament—Criticism, interpretation, etc. | Title.|
Classification: BS1692 2018 2018 (paperback) | BS1692 (ebook)

Manufactured in the U.S.A.   03/16/18

New Revised Standard Version Bible, copyright 1989, Division of Christian Education of the National Council of the Churches of Christ in the United States of America. Used by permission. All rights reserved.

Scripture quotations from The Authorized (King James) Version. Rights in the Authorized Version in the United Kingdom are vested in the Crown. Reproduced by permission of the Crown's patentee, Cambridge University Press

For my parents, they taught me almost everything
—now I can return the favor.

For my brother Paul, he taught me extreme walking.

Contents

WALKS

1. Heaven | 3
2. Satan | 22
3. The Messiah | 42
4. The Messiah Again | 58
5. The Hereafter | 78
6. Melchizedek | 98
7. Spirits | 120

BREAKS

A. My Brother Paul | 1
B. Extrabiblical Books | 19
C. How We Got the Canon | 37
D. The Deuterocanonical Books | 54
E. Pseudepigraphy | 74
F. The Dead Sea Scrolls | 94
G. Bible Translations | 115
H. Quite the Trip | 136

Bibliography 137
More Extreme Walking 139

A. My Brother Paul

One of my brothers is named Paul. He enjoys life. There never is a moment that he cannot free up for something exciting, but he never has time for boring things. My parents still talk about the greatest miracle that they have ever witnessed: Paul completing high school. Paul is so busy enjoying the small things that he forgets to work on useless things like money or his career. He's too busy smelling the roses to care that he's off the beaten path.

Naturally, he is my hero.

Paul has many more peculiarities. He refused to wear shoes until we moved to a country where it regularly froze. He would go barefoot everywhere—school, town, university, church. He wasn't able to survive in the Northern European climate of deadlines and clothing restrictions, so he moved to the Canary Islands. The Spanish culture of doing things *mañana*, without specifying *which mañana*, suits him perfectly.

Paul also really likes to go on walks, but no one wants to go with him. At least . . . not a second time. On the weekends, when his wife suggests they go for a walk, his daughters will always ask: "Are you choosing the route, or is Dad?" The reason for this is that Paul doesn't like paths. They are boring, because they are known. He's seen them already. When you go on a walk with Paul, his exploratory spirit takes over. He sees interesting and exciting things in the distance: a mountaintop, a tree, an odd-shaped rock. Interesting things that, of course, are very far away from the walkers, and far away from any type of path. Paul sees these things and cannot curtail his curiosity. He simply has to walk there.

So, there we would go. A left turn into the ravine. Keep on straight through the swamp. None of that matters! There is something interesting just ahead. If you go walking with Paul, you know for certain that you will return with dirty clothing, and probably with some minor wounds too.

Naturally, you will be absolutely exhausted. One time we were even arrested! But you also know that you will never again see the places you used to go to in the same light. Your worldview will have changed, forever.

Walking with Paul is not necessarily what I would call fun. It's exhausting, tiring, and terrifying. It is also very hard work. But you go anyway, because you see more than you would ever have thought possible. It is more impressive, more powerful than you ever could have imagined. As you grab adventure by the hand, step off the road and leave all well-known paths behind, you see things better. You experience things more deeply. In the end, you enjoy things much more.

This book is about being a Paul. Not as a walker (though I would surely advise doing that sometime too), but as a Christian and a theologian. As Christians, we know the Bible well, some of us know it very well. That is the path we walk over our entire lives. And, let's be clear, there is nothing wrong with that. That path is familiar, it is safe, and it leads us closer to Jesus. But, what happens if we look outside of the path? Are there any odd-shaped rocks, interesting trees, inviting mountaintops? Yes, there are: in this case other books written by Jews and Christians in the same times. These books are sources of additional knowledge and understanding. Do we need to be afraid that we will lose our way if we go out on discovery? By no means! We will experience things in a new way, and we needn't fear. The path is always near and safety is always just one bookcase away. We might take a longer route, and we might even have to cross a swamp, but we will always end up on the path, at the Bible.

In this book, we will walk together. We will see things—just as Paul does—in the distance, and then we will have to step off the path and head that way. We will be curious. We will go on a voyage of discovery. We will boldly explore far away from any paths, even if it means we return home tired, bruised, and maybe even with a minor scratch or two. We will return as changed people, no longer able to look at where we have been with the same eyes.

There! I see something interesting, not far off the path. I'm going to explore. Join me?

1. Heaven

A while ago I heard a joke about heaven. It makes fun of bus drivers and pastors. There is a long queue at the pearly gates. Saint Peter is there with his golden keys and the heavenly sign-in sheet, allocating eternal housing. The quality of your housing depends on how many holy deeds you did on earth, i.e., how many treasures you stored up in heaven. John, a pastor, is in the queue. He has worked his entire life for his calling. John spent seventy, eighty, ninety hours a week, every week, toiling for the Lord. John has certain expectations for his housing. Bored, John talks to the man in front of him; "Why not," he thinks, "the queue is very long." That man is a bus driver, he is obviously not as holy as a pastor.

Finally, after waiting what feels like an eternity it is the bus driver's turn. Saint Peter says "Look. There in the distance. Do you see that mountain? Do you see that huge white palace on top of the mountain? That's your house."

John, the pastor, starts to rub his hands together in delight. "If a bus driver gets a palace, what kind of place will I get!" he thinks. Smiling from ear to eternal ear he steps up to Peter.

"John, do you see that mountain over there?"
"Yes . . ."
"That mountain much larger than the bus driver's?"
"Yes!"
"Do you see that valley next to it? The one in constant shade?"
"Yes . . ."
"Do you see that lean-to that's almost falling apart?"
". . . yes . . ."
"Well, that is your house."

"What!? Why? How come? Why does a bus driver get a palace and I get a shack? I worked my entire life for God, I sacrificed all my evenings and weekends!" shouts John, who clearly has some issues with the heavenly housing allocation policies.

"Well, John, the problem is this. When you were preaching, everyone was sleeping, but when the bus driver was driving, everyone was praying harder than ever before."

Why write down this joke? Well, laughter is the best medicine. But, it also shows us a certain view of heaven. We have heard that heaven has gates, and that Saint Peter is often portrayed at them. We know that there is housing, and that many believe that what you do on earth influences what you get in heaven. I'm not saying that you or I believe this, or that it is correct, just that we have heard of these ideas before. Apparently, we understand exactly what is happening, otherwise this joke would not be funny.

This is an image that we have in our head. If I had written that this was a joke about a leopard and bus driver at the pearly gates, you would have been intrigued. You would have thought, "What? A leopard at the gates of heaven?" What if it wasn't Peter at the gates, but some terrible person from history? That too would have been strange. The joke itself is funny because it is very close to what we expect, but just a little bit different. Ninety percent is logical and obvious, and the peculiar ten percent makes the joke funny. By playing with our expectations a good story is created.

What I just explained is true for many things. Jokes, stories, movies, art—even the Bible. Jesus does exactly this when he preaches. Often he says, "you have heard . . . but I say." He says, for example, "You have heard 'you shall not murder,' but I say do not get angry" (Matthew 5:21–22). What is he doing? He is playing with expectations. Now, try to imagine that Jesus didn't say "you have heard." Try to imagine that we didn't even know what the people "had heard." Would we understand Jesus correctly? Would we know what his message was, if we didn't know the expectations, the context? We would not. To truly appreciate the bits that are different, we have to understand what they are different to.

In other words, if we want to understand "heaven" in the Bible, we have to know more than just the Bible.

1. Heaven

OUR IMAGE OF HEAVEN

I grew up as a Christian. In other words, I grew up with an image of heaven. Mine might be like yours. The image of heaven I grew up with is something like this: Everyone looks happy, healthy, and clean. No one has acne. In fact, everyone looks very smart in a generic sixties kind of way: men and boys in dark suits and ties, women and girls in dresses, and everyone has neat, if slightly outdated, hairdos. And, of course, everyone has a black-and-gold Bible under their arms. There are lions sitting next to lambs, and there are children playing with both. Everything is very green and very clean.

This is, in a nutshell, the image of heaven I grew up with. Through the years this image has changed a bit, but I still carry this nostalgic image in my head. I seriously doubt my hair will ever part as neatly as the hair in those pictures, but who knows, miracles do happen!

We all have an image of heaven—a picture in our heads that we have compiled through the years. Christians base their images mainly on the Bible (at least I should hope so). But what did the Bible writers base theirs on? Where did the authors of the New Testament get their image of heaven from? Some of it came from the Old Testament, some of it came from elsewhere. John tells of some visions he had of heaven in Revelation, but that was long after Matthew, Mark, Peter, and Paul had written their books. They didn't get their image of heaven from visions. They probably got it from the same place I got the dark suits and black-and-gold Bibles: general ideas that are common to their religion and culture. What then was their image of heaven?[1] Let's see.

Paul's Worldview

Maybe you think that this whole discussion is irrelevant. Maybe you think that the authors of the Bible had the same view of heaven as we do. Unfortunately for us that is absolutely not true. And I am not only talking about the dark suits. The differences are much larger than that! Let me give you

---

1. Just to be clear, in this chapter we are not talking about the place people immediately go when they die. For many Christians, these two places are the same, at least for the good people, but there is a difference for the authors of the New Testament. Heaven is the place where God lives and where humanity will live after judgement day; the hereafter is the place where humanity waits for that judgement. We will look at the hereafter later in this book.

an example. Paul writes something very intriguing in 2 Corinthians. In his letter he suddenly talks about someone in the "third heaven":

> It is necessary to boast; nothing is to be gained by it, but I will go on to visions and revelations of the Lord. I know a person in Christ who fourteen years ago was caught up to the third heaven—whether in the body or out of the body I do not know; God knows. And I know that such a person—whether in the body or out of the body I do not know; God knows—was caught up into Paradise and heard things that are not to be told, that no mortal is permitted to repeat. (2 Corinthians 12:1–4)

This is a peculiar passage. Paul says that he will discuss visions and revelations, and tells us of the experiences of a certain person that he knew. This person was taken up into the third heaven. He was even taken up into paradise. There he heard things that humans should not, or cannot, speak of.

This sounds strange to me. In my worldview, there is no third heaven. There is one heaven and God lives there. I will live there too someday, where I will have that nice suit and neat hair. Paul's view of heaven must be different to mine. How else could Paul talk of a third heaven?

Many writings from Paul's time describe multiple heavens. People explain how they were taken by an angel and given a heavenly tour. The people who get to see the heavens are always the holiest ones: heroes of the faith like Abraham, Isaac, Job, Enoch, and Levi. They are very important people. In other words, if you can report of a trip to heaven, you are clearly a religiously important person. These religious VIPs often visit multiple heavens, usually there are seven heavens. Most holy things come in sevens, so why not the heavens? And because God is the most holy, he lives in the seventh heaven: the highest heaven.

Having read this, do you feel like my brother Paul? Do you see something there, just a bit off the path? Something about heavens? Something you just have to see? Let's go and explore.

LEVI SEES THE SEVEN HEAVENS

> And behold, the heavens opened, and an angel of the Lord said to me, Levi, come in. And I went from the first heaven into the second; and I saw there water hanging between the two. And I saw

1. Heaven

a third heaven, far brighter and more brilliant than these two, and infinite in height. (*Testament of Levi* 2:6–8)[2]

This is a short passage from the *Testament of Levi*. We know of this book thanks to the tireless efforts of copyists through the ages, and we found parts of this book among the Dead Sea Scrolls. They are the last words of Levi, the son of Jacob. Levi's final testament to his sons. At least, that is what the work says that it is. It is very unlikely that Levi actually wrote this book, which is why we call this book pseudepigraphical. The term means "a writing falsely attributed to someone."

Leaving the author behind, in the passage above we read that Levi has been invited for a trip to heaven, with stops along the way. An angel lets him have a look at the heavens. Most importantly, not only is he allowed to see the heavens, he can actually enter them. A little bit later in his testament he describes his trip, heaven by heaven. He starts at the beginning:

Hear, then, about the seven heavens. The lowest is the gloomiest because it witnesses all the unrighteous deeds of men. (*Testament of Levi* 3:1b)

Intriguing! The heaven closest to us is gloomy, because it is closest to humanity's injustice. In other words, it's closest to the darkness of sin (see John 1:4–5). That's quite logical, when you think about it. Another reason it is gloomy is because this heaven is furthest away from God, who we all know is light. The first heaven is gloomy, the second one is full of weather:

The second [heaven] holds fire, snow, ice, ready for the day which the Lord has decreed in the righteous judgement of God: in it are all the spirits of retribution for vengeance on the wicked. (*Testament of Levi* 3:2)

The second heaven contains fire, snow, and ice. That snow and ice exist in the heavens is quite normal to people living in the colder parts of this world. Some places have months of snow every year, but for someone in Israel snow was by no means normal. Snow or ice from the sky was a disaster: exactly the same as fire from the sky. God often uses fire to destroy sinners, he could also use snow or ice (Genesis 19:24).

Here, in this second heaven, are the extreme weather conditions that can only be acts of God. So, when God wants to destroy a city, what does

---

2. All quotes from the *Testament of Levi* are from Jonge, "The Testaments of the Twelve Patriarchs."

he do? Simple. He lets some of these heavenly stores fall upon the earth. We might think this is too simplistic, but at the same time it makes a certain type of sense. The reasoning has a certain elegance.

What else is in this second heaven? Spirits (i.e., angels) who punish the wicked. This is harder to understand. Not many people nowadays would say that angels punish people, demons do that in hell. It might help to notice that the angels only punish the evil people, the wicked. When God stops time, when God finally destroys all evil, these angels are the ones responsible for the wicked, for the people who do not want to know God. The angels of punishment stand at the ready in the second heaven.

That is the second heaven, and Levi continues upward:

> In the third are the warrior hosts appointed to wreak vengeance on the spirits of error and of Beliar at the day of judgement. (*Testament of Levi* 3:3a)

The third heaven is similar to the second. Once again there are armies of angels, but these angels will attack Beliar (another name for Satan, 2 Corinthians 6:15) and his spirits. In the great, final battle between good and evil, these angels will fight on the side of good (see Revelation 19:11–21). They will destroy the evil angels, and they will avenge all the ages of misery that these evil spirits caused.

In order to achieve their mission, the warrior hosts need to be ready to attack. So here they are in the third heaven, just above the snow, ice, and fire. As close to humanity as possible, so that there needn't be any waiting.

Higher Heavens

Levi's trip continues with the fourth, fifth, sixth, and seventh heavens:

> But the heavens down to the fourth above these are holy [. . . .] And in the [fourth] heaven next to it are thrones and powers, in which praises are offered to God continually. (*Testament of Levi* 3:3b, 8)

Levi doesn't give us much information about the fourth heaven. What we do see is that there are heavenly thrones and powers. All of these thrones aren't for God; he doesn't even live in the fourth heaven. It is not entirely clear what or who these heavenly kings are who have these heavenly thrones. They are not the archangels, because they are higher up. Soon we will run into the archangels.

1. Heaven

While the heavenly kings might be a bit of a mystery, we do see heavenly rulers every now and then in the New Testament. Paul talks about powers, authorities, rulers, and dominions that are not earthly (Colossians 2:10, Ephesians 1:21, Romans 8:28). These heavenly powers, whatever they are, live in the fourth heaven—at least according to Levi. They do more than just ruling; they spend most of their time praising God without ceasing.

By this time, halfway through the heavens, we see that the heavens have become holy. There is no more talk of sin or punishment. These things are no longer discussed. We have started to move on to praising and holiness. And the fifth heaven is even more holy, it is filled with angels:

> And in the heaven below it [i.e., the fifth heaven] are the angels who bear the answers to the angels of the Lord's presence. (*Testament of Levi* 3:7)

The word "angel" in Greek just means "messenger." We have taken the Greek word for messenger "*angellos*" and bastardized it to "angel." We then stopped translating the Greek into English. We do this quite often: Christ (*christos* means anointed), synagogue (*synagoge* means gathering), Satan (*satanas* means adversary). Despite that the word "bastardize" sounds quite harsh, there is nothing wrong with this practice. Christ is not just any anointed person and an angel is much more than an earthly messenger. But, as we read the Bible we should always remind ourselves of these original meanings.

An angel was originally a messenger between God and humanity. The angels that went among humankind were exposed to the sins of humanity. This means that these angels would have been seen as unclean—just like the first heaven was unclean. These messenger angels were too unclean to enter the presence of God. That's why they could only reach the fifth heaven. There they could, as it were, shout up to the sixth heaven. The angels of the presence of God, who are in the sixth heaven, can hear them:

> And in the heaven next to it [i.e., the sixth] are the angels of the Lord's presence, who minister and make expiation to the Lord for all the sins committed unwittingly by the righteous: and they offer to the Lord a soothing odour, a spiritual and bloodless offering. (*Testament of Levi* 3:5–6)

In the sixth heaven, we see a special type of angel: the angels of the presence of the Lord. Literally the testament speaks of "the angels of the face of the Lord." Often these angels are called archangels (Revelation 8:1).

The Bible only ever calls one archangel by name—Michael (Jude 9)—and tells us that he is one of the chief princes (Daniel 10:13). Gabriel, another famous angel, is called an angel of the presence in the Bible, never an archangel (Luke 1:19). Outside of the Bible, Gabriel, Rafael, Uriel, and Jeremiel are often called archangels.

These angels do three things that are all related: they minister, they make expiation for humanity's sins, and they offer sacrifices. In this respect, they look very much like the Old Testament priests, who—just like these angels—ministered in the temple, made atonement for the sins of the people, and brought sacrifices to the Lord. It seems that the Jews and Christians back then imagined that there was a temple in heaven, just like on earth, where angels organized similar services to those in the earthly temple. This is not totally unexpected, whoever reads Hebrews 8 and 9 would come to a similar conclusion.

What is unexpected, however, is the sacrifice the archangels bring. This is a sacrifice with two characteristics: it is a spiritual or rational offering, and it is a bloodless offering. The first characteristic, "spiritual," is something that Paul also talks about (Romans 12:1). It is "spiritual" or "true" worship that we ourselves give to God. The other characteristic, "bloodless," is stranger. If you think about it carefully, a bloodless sacrifice is hard to imagine. On the other hand, you can imagine that a bloody offering is equally hard to imagine in heaven. Nowhere do we read "and this is where the bulls and lambs are kept for the sacrifices." There are no sacrificial animals in heaven, patiently awaiting their fate. In fact, there isn't any death at all in heaven. So, these archangels have to be sacrificing something else, something that wouldn't die. Something spiritual, something without blood. What that is exactly, the testament does not tell us. Maybe it is a good and godly life, just like in Romans 12. Maybe the angels' lifestyles *are* the sacrifice, or maybe it is something else altogether.

The Highest Heaven

God lives above the sixth heaven, in the seventh and highest heaven. The seventh heaven is a very holy place:

> For in the highest of all the Great Glory dwells, in the holy of holies, far above all holiness. (*Testament of Levi* 3:4)

1. Heaven

God lives far above all creation, above even the highest angels. It seems as if the author doesn't have words to describe how holy the seventh heaven is. The language has to become strange and awkward to even get close to describing God properly: he lives in the holy of holies, far above all holiness. That is how holy God is, how holy the place where he lives is.

A bit later Levi describes the seventh heaven in more detail:

> And the angel opened to me the gates of heaven, and I saw the holy temple, and the Most High sitting on a throne of glory. (*Testament of Levi* 5:1)

God sits on a throne of glory in the highest heaven. There is also a temple in the seventh heaven. So God sits on a throne next to, or inside of, a temple. This must be the original pattern that Moses copied when he built the earthly sanctuary (Exodus 25:9). The heavenly temple has not been made by human hands. A temple, where—we might assume—no one, not even the archangels, is worthy of ministering.

That concludes Levi's trip through the heavens, there and back again, from the first heaven to the seventh. We joined him, looking over the shoulders of ancient readers, and had our own voyage of discovery. We started in 2 Corinthians, where Paul tells us that he knows someone who went to the third heaven. And here, in the *Testament of Levi*, we discovered new knowledge of the ideas that Jews and Christians in those days had about heaven.

BACK TO PAUL

Should we, based on the *Testament of Levi*, conclude that there really are seven heavens? Should we believe that some man named Levi, many thousands of years ago, went on a trip all the way to the seventh heaven? You could, but I wouldn't. That is by no means why we went on this voyage of discovery. We want to use this extrabiblical knowledge to understand the Bible better. We are not looking for ideas that we can add to the Bible, but ideas that can help us place the Bible better. We want to broaden our horizons and broaden our understanding of the Bible. We are looking for new perspectives on the well-worn paths of the Bible.

We started our trip with a couple of intriguing sentences written by Paul. Let's return there now (2 Corinthians 12:1–4). The church in Corinth had some issues and Paul seems to have written quite a few letters to this church. We have two of these letters in the New Testament, and we know that there was at least one more (2 Corinthians 2:4). In Corinthians 12, Paul reacts to a big problem in Corinth. Other teachers are comparing themselves to Paul, and Paul's status is dropping fast.

The teachers are boasting. They say: "Look how amazing we are" and "Look at Paul, he's nowhere near as good as we are!" Not only are they boasting, they are smart about it. Never do they claim that they are richer or smarter than Paul. They only brag about how holy they are and how close to God they are. They know what could influence the Corinthians, and they know what was attractive to them: visions and tongues.

Speaking in tongues was already an issue in Corinth, we know this because Paul wrote to them about that earlier (1 Corinthians 14). Paul doesn't like these very exuberant signs of the Spirit. He much prefers it when churchgoers talk about God in a way others can understand, rather than shouting incomprehensible gibberish (1 Corinthians 14:5). This is not to say that Paul couldn't speak in tongues. He has that gift better than anyone (1 Corinthians 14:18). He can speak in tongues; he just feels that it is useless in a worship service.

The boasting teachers in Corinth could probably speak in tongues with the best of them. They constantly brag about the visions that they receive from God. Their actions are all geared towards showing how incredibly holy they are. Poor Paul has not been in Corinth for months, and thanks to these teachers he has been pushed to the back of everyone's minds. He's losing touch with the brothers and sisters in Corinth. But he is not worried about his status, as a good pastor he is worried about the salvation of the Corinthians, he is worried that they will end up going the wrong way. He reacts to these boasting teachers in a long letter. A letter steeped in irony.

A Little Bit of Irony Never Hurt Anyone

> I wish you would bear with me in a little foolishness. Do bear with me! (2 Corinthians 11:1)

Paul is about to get foolish. Just like those boasters, he too is going to brag. He tells the Corinthians that he is absolutely not inferior to the "super-apostles" in Corinth (2 Corinthians 11:5). He has more than enough knowledge, he proclaims God's good news, and he has always been self-sufficient (2 Corinthians 11:6–11).

1. Heaven

Now Paul gets even more foolish. He's going to compare himself to these super-apostles even more (2 Corinthians 11:21–28). Are these teachers Hebrews? So is Paul. Are they Israelites, descendants of Abraham? So is Paul! Are they ministers of Christ? Paul is more. Paul has worked harder, he has spent more time in prison. He has had more beatings and floggings. He has been shipwrecked more often, been hungry more often, been thirsty more often. Not to mention the psychological pressure of ministering to dozens of churches. These teachers can boast, but Paul can boast more … and it's all true!

In the middle of Paul's foolish boasting, we arrive at the passage that sent us out on this voyage of discovery. Here Paul suddenly boasts of the third heaven. Paul does not want to boast, but these other teachers have made it necessary. He simply has to fight fire with fire, otherwise the members in Corinth will no longer listen to him—a real apostle, as opposed to these newcomers. Just as Satan disguised himself as an angel of light, these teachers disguise themselves as ministers of Christ (2 Corinthians 11:13–14). To counteract these false ministers Paul has been bragging for a while, and now he adds to it:

> It is necessary to boast; nothing is to be gained by it, but I will go on to visions and revelations of the Lord. I know a person in Christ who fourteen years ago was caught up to the third heaven—whether in the body or out of the body I do not know; God knows. And I know that such a person—whether in the body or out of the body I do not know; God knows—was caught up into Paradise and heard things that are not to be told, that no mortal is permitted to repeat. On behalf of such a one I will boast, but on my own behalf I will not boast, except of my weaknesses. (2 Corinthians 12:1–5)

Humble Boasting

The Corinthians are interested in visions and revelations. Their teachers have been boasting about their visions and therefore Paul must too. He says he knows "someone" who went all the way to the third heaven. We could wonder who this someone was. Up till now Paul has been boasting about himself. It would be very illogical if Paul were suddenly boasting about his friends. But at the same time he has been very clear that Christians should not boast. So, he tries to be humble and to boast at the same time:

He introduces this "someone" about whom he will boast. In all humility, he can boast about "someone" because it is not himself. But everyone who reads this will know that this "someone" is none other than Paul himself. Think of it as a way for Paul to do what is necessary, even though he has ethical issues with it.

Paul has been taken up into heaven. He received the heavenly tour, just like Levi did. A heavenly visit is a very special revelation, an extraordinary vision. You have to be someone special to be invited to see heaven. Paul shows that he is part of a very select group. He has added his name to the list of VIPs: Moses, Abraham, Levi, Enoch, and Isaac—not bad company.

Paul didn't just visit though; he must have also seen things in heaven. He seems unwilling to talk about what he saw. Levi discussed the details extensively, but Paul gives none. This is probably because the *Testament of Levi* was never intended to be a revelation of God. It was written, just like Christian books are written nowadays, to help its contemporaries to think and discuss faith and heaven. Back then you did that by narrating visions, even if you had just made those up. The author never actually had that vision, he is only speculating on what may or may not be in heaven.

Paul is a different case. I strongly doubt that Paul is just making this vision up. Why would he be lying *and* boasting, when he was so against boasting in the first place? He knows what he has seen. He has experienced something, and has learnt something, that need not and should not be shared. Paul is not speculating about what may or may not be in heaven. He is only sharing that he saw heaven. He has no intentions of teaching about heaven; he only wants to keep his church members on the right path . . . and to remind them not to boast. He gives them just enough information to show that he was taken up by God, but nothing more or less. Quite a pity from our point of view as we would have loved to have some more information!

HEBREWS

Paul is not the only biblical author who speaks of the heavens. The author of Hebrews—who was almost definitely not Paul—seems to be interested in the heavens as well.[3] Hebrews is known as a tricky book to understand.

---

3. Many pages and much ink has been spent discussing the author of Hebrews. The book itself is anonymous, but many people assumed and still assume that it was written by Paul. A comparison of style and theology between Paul's letters and Hebrews shows

1. Heaven

The author of this book is smart and scholarly: he's good with theology and he's good with words too. He was a theologian and a good writer (or, more likely, a good orator). His language stands out in the New Testament because it is very literary. Similarly, his theology stands out, as unique within the New Testament. The idea that Jesus is a high priest comes solely from this book.

You could summarize the book of Hebrews like this: "Jesus is better than everything and everyone." That might sound a bit simplistic, but all summaries are. Hebrews gets its name from the fact that it seems to be written to Jews (i.e., Hebrews). So, it was written for people who did not believe in Jesus, but did believe in God and in the Old Testament. That means that the book attempts to convince its audience to believe in Jesus.

Hebrews gets right to it. In what is considered the most literary introduction to any Bible book, it immediately begins with Jesus. While it was great that God spoke to people via prophets, God was able to speak much better via Jesus the Son (Hebrews 1:1–4). Jesus is higher than any and everything, higher even than the angels (Hebrews 1:5–14). If we were to import Levi's descriptions of the heavens into this passage, we could say that even the archangels were only allowed to rise to the sixth heaven, but Jesus could go all the way to the seventh. Jesus is worshipped by the angels (Hebrews 1:6) and sits at God's right hand (Hebrews 1:13).

Jesus is a High Priest

Having proven that Jesus is the best of the best, Hebrews sets out to show what the link is between Jesus, salvation, and high priesthood. This is the topic that Hebrews wants to address. Jesus was the highest and put himself among the lowest. He became like us in "every respect, so that he might be a merciful and faithful high priest in the service of God, to make a sacrifice of atonement for the sins of the people" (Hebrews 2:17). He is faithful because he humiliated himself; he is merciful because he has endured what we endure—he understands us! And through his death he achieved salvation for all people.

After this wonderful explanation and defence of Jesus, Hebrews shifts to a discussion of faith and trust (Hebrews 3:1—4:14). Faith and trust from our side leads to salvation; unbelief and distrust leads to death. The story of the Israelites in the desert is included as an example. Ten of the twelve

---

that it is very unlikely that Paul wrote Hebrews. Who did write it is anyone's guess.

spies were too afraid to enter the promised land, because they did not have enough faith and trust in God. In conclusion, we, as believers, should not follow their example, but should cling to the faith. That last sentence of this discussion of faith and trust, includes the heavens:

> Since, then, we have a great high priest who has passed through the heavens, Jesus, the Son of God, let us hold fast to our confession. (Hebrews 4:14)

Maybe we would have quickly read on, past this sentence, but after exploring the seven heavens with Levi, we should immediately see something important. "Heavens" is plural! Jesus didn't pass through one heaven, but he passed through all the heavens. We have a high priest who, after dying on the cross, passed through all seven heavens. He is back where he started: in the seventh heaven. And precisely this trip is what makes Jesus so useful as our redeemer and mediator. Jesus is back where God is.

It gets better. Hebrews says that the faithful will make exactly the same trip as Jesus (Hebrews 4:16). We are going back to God's presence. So, Hebrews has a view of heaven that requires a trip through all the heavens. This is a trip that not everyone will and can make. The angels get a bit more than halfway. The archangels make it all the way to the sixth. But Jesus, who is better than anyone and everything, makes it all the way to the top . . . and we can join him. Jesus and his voyage through the heavens is the reason we can "approach the throne of grace with boldness, so that we may receive mercy and find grace to help in time of need" (Hebrews 4:16).

In the subsequent chapters of Hebrews, the voyage through the heavens is discussed no less than five times (Hebrews 6:19–20; 8:1–2; 9:11, 24; 10:20). It is always in slightly oblique terms, but by no means invisible to us. At least, that is, if we are willing to think hard. So think with me. Hebrews is written to appeal to Jews. They know the sanctuary, either the tabernacle in the desert or the temple in Jerusalem. In fact, they know the sanctuary well. They know that the sanctuary consists of two parts: the holy and the holy of holies (or more correctly the holiest). Priests regularly enter the holy to minister to the Lord. But the holy of holies is another matter. Only the high priest is allowed in there, and he is only allowed there very seldom.

In heaven, there are services for the Lord too. Levi saw those in the sixth heaven: archangels who were doing priestly duties. Could we then conclude that the sixth heaven is comparable to the holy? It seems logical that the heavenly sanctuary, on which the earthly one is based, also has two

1. Heaven

parts. It is a small logical leap to assume that if the sixth heaven is like the holy, the seventh heaven is like the holy of holies.

Past the Curtain

Once we have made it this far, we only need to make one more small step. In the earthly sanctuary, there is a curtain between the Holy and the Holy of Holies, sometimes called the "veil." Whether or not there is a curtain in heaven is unimportant for this discussion. It is the symbolism that is important. Passing the curtain is symbolic for entering the Holy of Holies. Once you have passed the curtain, you truly are in the seventh heaven.

Keeping this in mind, suddenly the passages of Jesus' trip through the heavens becomes much more vivid. Hebrews 6 calls Jesus our hope:

> We have this hope, a sure and steadfast anchor of the soul, a hope that enters the inner shrine behind the curtain, where Jesus, a forerunner on our behalf, has entered, having become a high priest forever according to the order of Melchizedek. (Hebrews 6:19–20)

Jesus is our hope. He is dependable, he is our anchor. He has gone ahead, even beyond the curtain, into the "inner shrine." He has passed the sixth heaven, past the limit for the angels, into the seventh. This is the foundation of the gospel in Hebrews. Hebrews wants to make this so clear that it is repeated four more times (Hebrews 8:1–2; 9:11, 24; and 10:20).

Jesus is in God's presence. He has gone ahead. We too will rise up, passing through the six heavens all the way into the seventh, into the very presence of God.

IMAGES REVISITED

There are more places in the Bible where you can see that multiple heavens are on the author's mind. Take Revelation 8:1, where the heavens become silent. Is that to ensure that there is no noise in the heavens between God and earth? What about Jesus' triumphal entrance into Jerusalem, where the people shout "Hosanna in the highest heaven!" (Matthew 21:9; Mark 11:10). This view of heavens must explain why Jesus almost never talks of the kingdom of heaven (as most English Bibles read) but of the kingdom of the heavens.

The New Testament refers to "the heavens" about ninety times. Should we then conclude that there literally are seven physical heavens? I don't think that is useful. How heaven looks or scientifically functions goes far beyond our understanding. Some people in the time of the New Testament imagined that heaven consisted of seven heavens. That is their image of heaven. I have a different view and different expectations. I am sure you have different ones too. What heaven is like, no one really knows. But whatever you think, God lives there so it must be great.

It is not strange that people in the time of the Bible had a different view of heaven than we do. By studying their views, we get a better understanding of what Paul means when writing about the third heaven. He used this to counteract the teachings of false apostles, and to show that he too had something to reluctantly boast about.

Now that we know about the seven heavens, we have a much better understanding of Jesus' heavenly trip, as we read of it in Hebrews. Jesus went through the curtain, through the penultimate heaven, all the way to the final one. He went into the very presence of God, to a place that even the angels cannot enter. And the best part? We can go there too, following where Jesus went before.

We saw something interesting next to our path. Just there, close by. Another image of the heavens. We went out exploring and returned to the path, with a richer understanding, with better information, and with deeper context. Not bad, for a day's work. Now, we need to take a break.

We need to get our breath back. Just a small breather. We will do that after every walk: take a short break and discuss something else. This break will be about extrabiblical books.

B. Extrabiblical Books

Christians are very focused on the Bible. There is nothing wrong with that. When Christians speak of the Bible, however, confusion can arise. Somewhere in history we agreed on a canon, meaning we agreed on the actual contents of the Bible. When most Protestants refer to "the Bible," they mean a certain sixty-six books in the Old and New Testaments. These books together are often called Scripture or the Word of God. Christians consider these books to be inspired.

Almost all Christians know that there are more books from the time of the Bible. In some Bibles you might see nine books printed between the Old and New Testament. These are called the deuterocanonical (second canon) or apocryphal (hidden) books. The sixty-six–book canon is not the only one: the Catholic canon has more books, seven or nine, depending how you count. We will discuss these books in more detail later.

What most Christians don't know is that the deuterocanonical books are just the tip of the iceberg. Some Ethiopian churches have fifteen additional books in their canon, but even that doesn't include all the books out there. There are hundreds of Jewish and Christian books from the time of the Bible. Very few people actually know what is in all these books. In fact, most Christians are likely to ignore them, because they don't consider them to be part of inspired Scripture.

Uninspired

Inspiration is a complicated topic. Let's think about it for a moment: is the daily devotional we read inspired? What about latest book by a famous Christian author? Or that textbook on economics? Is the newspaper inspired? What about the news on TV? None of these are inspired like the

Bible is, but we don't just ignore them. They contain valuable information that we need to have. When we ignore ancient Jewish and Christian sources, we miss out on a treasure trove of useful information. I find that very strange. Most of us would agree that archaeology and history are vital to understanding the Bible. As good students of the Bible, we should not ignore these extrabiblical books either. They can help us to understand the Bible so much better.

There are two ways that these books can strengthen our faith and inform our theology. The first has to do with the large amount of time between the Old and New Testaments. If all the Old Testament books were written by the people they are ascribed to, we are talking about a span of at least five hundred years. Even if we assume the books were written by their followers, there are still centuries between the two testaments.

Consider the last three centuries of world history. Think of the great literature that has been written, the changes in culture and philosophy, the various religions that have gained and lost ground. Consider the countries that have been founded or have disappeared. Imagine trying to ignore all of that. What would you misunderstand because you lack the correct information? Let me put that the other way around: if you were to time travel from 1717 to 2017 would you understand *anything* correctly? If we ignore these writings, which are often the only witness to ancient culture that we still have, we miss out on huge amounts of information. Sometimes, we understand the New Testament poorly because of this.

Consider the differences between the Old and the New Testament. Satan is hardly in the Old Testament (just three times), and is present almost everywhere in the New Testament. Where does that emphasis on Satan come from? The Old Testament is silent about an afterlife: the dead know nothing, feel nothing, experience nothing. The New Testament shows a different picture. There is an eternal fire (Mark 9:45–28) and Jesus makes a trip to the underworld (1 Peter 3:19). Where does this belief in a hell and underworld come from?

Discontinuity

In Biblical Studies, we call this logical leap discontinuity. That means that certain topics don't match up. We see discontinuity between the Old and the New Testament in some areas. Naturally, this discontinuity did not just appear out of nowhere. It is the result of hundreds of years of thinking,

B. Extrabiblical Books

believing, and writing. Sometimes this led people away from God's ideals—Jesus regularly renounces various doctrines. Other times it did not.

We are going to look at these extrabiblical books, but not to form a theology. We want to read them to understand the context—the background—of the inspired authors of the Bible, and to understand what they are reacting against. We will study them to better understand the worldviews present in the books.

First Test, Then Decide

That brings us to the second way these books can strengthen our faith and theology. Our interpretation of the Bible is very dependent on those who came before us. We know a lot about some earlier interpreters and very little about others. Who knows: by studying more theological ideas of early Christians, we might find something that helps us understand God's revelation even better. If we decide not to even look at these books, we have automatically decided that there is nothing useful in them, without even having explored the possibility.

Paul famously says "test everything; hold fast to what is good" (1 Thessalonians 5:21). This is a task for each of us. We can't just make assumptions; we can't just take other people's opinions for granted. Theology is a process of searching and researching, questioning and testing. In this book, we will take Paul's advice. We will discover what is outside of the Bible, and test it.

Trust me, we will see wonderful things.

2. Satan

Grab your Bible, and open it to the New Testament. You don't have to read very far before you run into Satan. The Devil is introduced right at the beginning of Jesus' ministry, and he immediately gets the name Satan (Matthew 4:1, 10). Matthew has a good reason for this. There is a strong connection between Jesus' redemptive work and Satan's existence.

Now, think about the fact the New Testament is called "new" because there is also an Old Testament. You would expect Satan to be a regular sight there too. Nothing is less true! If you read the Old Testament from cover to cover, all nine hundred pages in my Bible, you will run into this evil figure only three times (2 Chronicles 21:1; Job 1–2; Zechariah 3:1–2). That's once per three hundred pages.

This difference between the Old and New Testaments is intriguing. Satan is a frequent figure in the New Testament. If you read the New Testament cover to cover, only 250 pages, you will run into his name thirty-six times. If you include all the other names for Satan, such as devil, tempter, Beezeboul, Belial, and adversary, you end up with almost 140 times. In 250 pages, that is more than every other page!

Yes, I know that, if we do our best, we can find Satan a few more times in the Old Testament. The snake in Genesis: that has to be Satan. Right? And the prideful Lucifer, that's Satan too. We can recognize Satan in a few more places in the Old Testament, but we only recognize him because the New Testament has taught us so much about Satan. With Revelation in the back of our mind it suddenly becomes clear that the snake in Eden is Satan. But without the New Testament, we would have never associated the prideful angel Lucifer with Satan.

There is also a big difference between how the Old Testament and the New Testament portray Satan. This difference is significant if you consider the theological role that Satan plays for many people. Satan is not small or

2. SATAN

unimportant at all for a good deal of Christians. He is the great opponent of God and humanity.

We can attribute this difference to humanity's growing understanding and to God's growing revelation. Through the ages people learnt more and more about reality and God revealed more and more to them. This could be why Satan's role is so small in the Old Testament and suddenly so much larger in the New Testament. Maybe people in the time of Abraham were not ready to learn all about the great enemy, or maybe they had just not realized it yet. Maybe by the time the New Testament rolled around, they were ready to understand the nature of evil.

We could conclude that there has always been progress in how humanity understood God's grace and mercy, and salvation. That same progress can be seen with how humanity understood Satan. But, if we are honest, there seems to be quite a large gap between Satan of the Old and New Testament. Larger than for other topics. In fact, the gap is not just in how often we read about him, but also in what he does.

Do you feel exploration calling? Are you intrigued? Be patient, for just a little longer. We can't leave the path yet. Let's first look at the great tempter in more detail. What do we know about him?

SATAN, WHO WAS THAT AGAIN?

It is not hard to make a list of Satan's characteristics. We needn't even open the Bible. Satan is evil. He's a rebel. He used to be an angel, but he has fallen. He didn't want to listen to God because he was prideful and so he was thrown out of heaven. Disguised as a snake he tempted Eve, and thus sin was introduced into the world. He's still around and tempts each one of us.

We could say more, but this is a good general picture. Most Christians believe in this description, and most people who know anything about Satan will give you these—or very similar—details. It shouldn't be hard to find Bible verses that show us these characteristics, but if we look at the Old Testament we only see some parts of this image of Satan. Other parts are wholly missing. Let's look for Satan in the Old Testament.

Job is probably the oldest passage from the Bible discussing Satan. Job is an intriguing book that raises—at least for me—many questions. Job begins with a sort of United Nations in heaven. Satan is apparently the delegate from Earth. There, during a break in the meetings, he has a conversation with God. As regularly happens when you speak to someone from a different country, God asks: "Hey, Satan, you're from Earth, do you know Job?" And Satan does know him. Read what happens next:

> The Lord said to Satan, "Have you considered my servant Job? There is no one like him on the earth, a blameless and upright man who fears God and turns away from evil." Then Satan answered the Lord, "Does Job fear God for nothing? Have you not put a fence around him and his house and all that he has, on every side? You have blessed the work of his hands, and his possessions have increased in the land. But stretch out your hand now, and touch all that he has, and he will curse you to your face." The Lord said to Satan, "Very well, all that he has is in your power; only do not stretch out your hand against him!" So Satan went out from the presence of the Lord. (Job 1:8–12)

Quite a strange discussion. So strange in fact, that we sometimes don't see all the nuances. What happens exactly?

"Job is a good man," says God. "The best of the best. No one on earth is as righteous as he is. He is a true Believer, with a capital B. And best of all, he honors me above everything. He respects me. He loves me."

"Obviously!" Satan answers. "Look at what you have given him. You protect him. You protect his family and even his cattle! You bless everything he does. He just keeps getting richer and richer. No wonder he likes you!"

"Job doesn't believe because he is a good person," Satan continues. "Job believes because you make it worth his while. I bet you that he won't be faithful if you don't bless him anymore."

Now, God must know Job better than that, but he gives Satan the chance to test his theory. Job's children, his servants, and his cattle all die. But Job stays faithful to God.

Careful Examination

If we want to understand this narrative properly, we need to give it some careful examination. That means we must look at it as the original audience would have looked, using only this narrative as our reference. We can't include books written later, like Chronicles or the New Testament. We can't include our theology or what we have read in other books. That is a challenge, but let's try.

In this narrative, we see that God and Satan are talking to each other. Satan has not been banished from God's sight. He is allowed to enter

2. SATAN

heaven, to enter God's presence, and to talk to God. God says that Job is a good person, but Satan has his doubts. If we are honest, these doubts are not very hard to understand: if God gives you everything you desire, you might well believe *because* you get so much.

So, Satan suggests testing Job's faith. How? Does he want to tempt Job to do evil, like we would expect Satan to? Not at all. Satan does not want to tempt Job, he wants to take away some of Job's blessings. He wants to remove some things that Job did not necessarily deserve and see what happens to Job's faith.

Now I am the first to admit that what Satan does is not great. Not great for Job, absolutely not great for Job's family, servants, and cattle. But, if we are honest, does this passage show us Satan, the big rebel, who was thrown out of heaven? Do you see the Satan who tempts all of humanity to sin? Not really. He's a bit of a rebel, maybe, because he's not willing to take God's word that Job is righteous. But he does ask God for permission and does exactly what God allows him to do.

In the next chapter there is a second discussion in heaven. Satan wants to make life more challenging for Job. Again he gets God's permission, this time to hurt Job, as long as he does not kill him. The rest of the book of Job discusses Job's pain and struggles and how, no matter what, Job stayed faithful to God.

Let's draw some conclusions about Satan's role. And don't forget to put everything you know about Satan out of your head. My conclusion is that Satan tests Job and thus proves that Job truly believes. In other words, Satan vindicates Job.

That's a different conclusion to what we might have expected. And, let's be honest, maybe God is just using Satan to achieve a goal that Satan does not want at all. But, if we take this narrative as the introduction to the book of Job, we clearly see that it is Satan who provides the evidence that Job is—without any doubt—a good person.

A VERY DIFFERENT SATAN

This role for Satan is rather different to what we are used to from the New Testament. It is also very different to what you often hear in church or from theologians. Nevertheless, if we read more of the Old Testament, we actually see a similar role for Satan in Zechariah. In Zechariah 3, as an introduction to a baffling vision about Joshua and the Messiah, we see this passage:

> Then he showed me the high priest Joshua standing before the angel of the Lord, and Satan standing at his right hand to accuse him. And the Lord said to Satan, "The Lord rebuke you, O Satan! The Lord who has chosen Jerusalem rebuke you! Is not this man a brand plucked from the fire?" (Zechariah 3:1–2)

I imagine this as a court scene. We have the defendant, Joshua, we have an angel of the Lord, and we have Satan. Satan is standing at God's right hand to accuse the defendant. That seems very similar to what the public prosecutor does. Satan is not a tempter or the source of all evil. He's there to show the Lord what mistakes Joshua has made.

This is quite similar to Job. In Zechariah, a man who is righteous is proven righteous in a court case. Satan, as the prosecutor, attempts to show that Joshua is evil, but in the end Joshua is vindicated.

Apparently, the image of Satan as an evil tempter has not stuck among the Bible authors. Satan is an accuser, not a tempter. This is not very strange, because Satan is actually just a Hebrew word. It means accuser. In a wonderful tautology, Zechariah 3:1 literally reads "Satan standing at his right hand as satan." And, now that we have started with Hebrew, there is more to learn about Satan—or more precisely, satan.

In the narrative of Balaam we also run into Satan, just not in English. The story of Balaam is very entertaining to read; do that by all means. Start in Numbers 22; I will only discuss it very briefly. Balaam sets out to do something that God does not want him to do. Balaam knows that very well. He's riding along on his donkey and fleeing from God's will. That can never end well.

Suddenly the donkey starts acting up. It does not want to move forward. Balaam gets agitated and hits the donkey, to no avail. Eventually the donkey speaks and tells Balaam what is happening, and then Balaam realizes what is going on:

> God's anger was kindled because he was going, and the angel of the Lord took his stand in the road as his adversary. Now he was riding on the donkey, and his two servants were with him. (Numbers 22:22)

That is the English, but the Hebrew is very different. A literal translation could be "The angel of YHWH stood in the road as satan." That's right, Satan, the great figure of evil, in the same sentence as an angel of the Lord. That's quite something. An angel playing the role of Satan, at the very least a strange occurrence. What, then, does it mean?

2. SATAN

Progressive Understanding

As I wrote above, the Bible is full of progressive understanding. This is specially the case with Satan. As you read backwards from the New Testament, everything falls into place. But without the New Testament, you would have a completely different view of Satan. He is not portrayed as rebellious. At most he is the devil's advocate, testing the righteousness of individuals on God's behalf. He does not tempt people to sin, but does keep a close eye on everyone to see if they are sinning. Maybe from his point of view it would be a victory if someone were to sin, but his divine task is proving that people are righteous. He shows that a person will be faithful no matter what, just as he did with Job. The word "satan" itself is not even a bad word in some contexts. Even an angel can be a satan when doing God's bidding.

Now, I'm itching to step off the path. I see so many interesting things just out of reach. So many things that we can discover. Don't get me wrong—the Old Testament has already shown us many intriguing perspectives but, trust me, where we are going is even more intriguing. If you were paying attention, and if you have a good knowledge of the Old Testament, you know that I have skipped a passage. The final place that Satan appears is in Chronicles.

First and Second Chronicles are the newest books in the Old Testament. If what I have been saying about progressive understanding is correct, we should see some of that in this book. It should show us a glimpse of the further revelation of God in the Bible. And, don't worry, it does.

New and Improved Version

Chronicles is basically a retelling of the books of Samuel and Kings. You could call it *Samuel & Kings: The New and Improved Version*. Maybe we could compare it to a new Bible translation. When you read it, it feels a bit strange. The wording is different and unfamiliar, but often it is a lot easier to understand. Chronicles is the same: different and unfamiliar to Samuel and Kings, but often easier to understand. Read what 2 Samuel says and how Chronicles relates it:

> Again the anger of the Lord was kindled against Israel, and he incited David against them, saying, "Go, count the people of Israel and Judah." (2 Samuel 24:1)

> Satan stood up against Israel, and incited David to count the people of Israel. (1 Chronicles 21:1)

David is going to hold a census. It is not entirely clear to me why counting the Israelites is so bad. Maybe David was planning to use this information to boast about how many subjects he had, or maybe David didn't stick to the rules from the Torah for holding censuses. Whatever the reason, it is clearly very bad. Joab advises David not to count, and when David is done he is very sorry that he did.

In Samuel, David counts his people because God is angry. I can understand that God gets angry sometimes, but that God then makes David do something that both he and God regret is harder to understand. Especially if you read the rest of the chapter and see the terrible consequences of this census. This is even more mystifying if we consider that God is portrayed so lovingly in the New Testament. I find it hard to imagine that God does this. Apparently, so did the editor and author of Chronicles. They must have read this narrative and known that there was something else going on. Of course, it wasn't God who put David on this track of destruction, it had to be Satan. In their version, they fixed the theology.

Let us leave the Old Testament behind us now. In fact, let's step off that path and go exploring. As we walk, the undergrowth is getting thicker, the going is getting tougher. What do we see?

JUBILEES

> In the third week of that jubilee the polluted demons began to lead astray the children of Noah's sons and to lead them to folly and to destroy them. And the sons of Noah came to Noah, their father, and they told him about the demons who were leading astray and blinding and killing his grandchildren. And he prayed before the LORD his God and he said, "God of the spirits which are in all flesh, who has acted mercifully with me and saved me and my sons from the water of the Flood and did not let me perish as you did the children of perdition, because 'Great was your grace upon me, and great was your mercy upon my soul. Let your grace be lifted up upon my sons, and do not let the evil spirits rule over them, lest they destroy them from the earth. But bless me and my sons. And let us grow and increase and fill the earth.'"[1] (*Jubilees* 10:1–3)

---

1. All quotes from *Jubilees* are from Wintermute, "Jubilees."

2. SATAN

This passage is about demons that lead people astray, that blind and kill. They lead people to sin, they blind them from the truth, and they kill them. They don't personally kill people, but lead them to sin and its wages: death. They are evil demons that have nothing good in store for Noah and his family. Here is an image of the forces of darkness that is much closer to home. This is more like what we are used to, and very different to what we saw in the Old Testament.

The passage above is a part of *Jubilees*. This book was written about 200 BCE, probably by a priest or another theologically trained person. *Jubilees* fantasizes about what Moses saw when he was on Sinai for forty days (Exodus 24:18). In fifty chapters Moses writes down everything that the angel told him. Every single detail of history, from the very beginning at creation, all the way up to Moses's time. In *Jubilees* thousands of years of history are written down by Moses on mount Sinai. This is obviously not how *Jubilees* came to be, but it is a nice piece of fiction that fits into biblical history.

NOAH

After a while the angel starts to tell Moses about Noah. Noah has survived the flood and wants to get on with his new life on a clean earth. But all is not going according to plan. Demons are being irritating. They are messing things up for Noah and his family. They can't go a day without some demon or other coming along and pestering them. Finally it's the last straw, and the children come to complain to Noah.

Noah, the patriarch, is the person who has to pray to God. So he gets down on his knees. He reminisces about the time of the flood, and about how God's mercy saved him and his children from death. Then he asks for more mercy. He does not want the evil spirits to master his children. These spirits are clearly very dangerous, for if they lead his children astray, the children will be lost. Noah's prayer does not stop there. He continues:

> And you know that which your Watchers, the fathers of these spirits, did in my days and also these spirits who are alive. Shut them up and take them to the place of judgment. And do not let them cause corruption among the sons of your servant, O my God, because they are cruel and were created to destroy. And let them not rule over the spirits of the living because you alone know their

judgment, and do not let them have power over the children of the righteous henceforth and forever. (*Jubilees* 10:4-6)

Apparently Noah knows a lot about these spirits. He knows where they came from and he knows what their power is. The demons are children of something Noah calls "your Watchers." These Watchers were, if we can judge by Noah's tone, not the nicest people around. They must be very important: why else would Noah bring them up? So who, or what, are these Watchers?

THE WATCHERS

The Watchers are often discussed in extrabiblical books. The birthplace of all these discussions is an obscure passage in Genesis. Out of nowhere, the book talks about sons of God who see that the daughters of humanity are beautiful and marry them (Genesis 6:2). These sons of God have children with human women, and "the Nephilim were on the earth in those days" (Genesis 6:4). And the children of the sons of God and humanity are "the heroes that were of old, warriors of renown" (Genesis 6:4). In the very next verse, Genesis starts to discuss how incredibly evil humanity was, and then comes the flood. These Nephilim are only found in one other Bible verse, which calls the people in the promised land "Nephilim," or, as most translations read, "giants" (Numbers 13:33).

It should be quite apparent that this is not the easiest passage from the Bible to interpret. For centuries people have been interpreting it in different ways. Who are these sons of God? Are the Nephilim the fruit of the marriage between the sons of God and humankind? What does the word Nephilim even mean? Are they giants? What is the link between these four verses and the flood? All of these questions led to a huge, fantastical discussion outside of the Bible. You could find almost any interpretation, but the most common one goes something like this.

In Noah's time there were many angels on earth. They had been sent by God to watch over humanity. The angel with the flaming sword from Eden was the first of thousands. It was a great army, with angelic generals, but one angel was the supreme commander. This angel has many names such as Azazel, Semyaz, and Satanael.

These angels roamed the earth, amongst humanity. No problem there, were it not that women are so pretty. Some authors say that the women seduced the angels on purpose, using makeup and perfume. Others say that it was the angels who initiated the romance. Whatever the explanation, angels and women end up in bed together. This generally leads to offspring.

So, what does the child of an angel and a woman look like? Well, it can't be normal. Angels are beings of spirit, women are beings of flesh and blood. The offspring of this union must be very special. How? Well, it must be a giant! It's an angel-human hybrid, huge and impressive with supernatural powers: a hero. But, this was clearly not God's intention. Angels can't marry people, *people* marry people. Angels don't marry at all (Matthew 22:30). These are incredible sins against God's natural order. They are sins against God. These supernatural offspring must then be very evil. They were born out of sin, so they must be sinful. And if this is happening all around, clearly all of humanity was evil. Everyone, that is, except Noah—so God sent the flood, but Noah was saved.

And thus a tradition about the Watchers was born. They are angels who went against their nature and begat half-blood children. These children were semi-immortal. Their flesh would die, but their spirit would live on. They would become bodiless spirits who roam the earth, jealous of all living flesh, leading people to sin so that they too will die.

Please don't take this interpretation as a God-given truth. It is simply a common interpretation from New Testamental times—one of a few. It is useful for us, as it helps understand the background to the New Testament better.

Back to Noah in *Jubilees*

Now it should be a lot more understandable what Noah means when he says:

> And you know that which your Watchers, the fathers of these spirits, did in my days and also these spirits who are alive. Shut them up and take them to the place of judgment. (*Jubilees* 10:4)

The Watchers went against the natural order. They had sex with women: that is very evil. Their children, the spirits, still roam the earth and attack the righteous, and that too is evil. These spirits deserve judgement, and need to be shut up right now.

Fortunately, God listens to Noah. He decides to destroy the spirits, but before God can execute his decision, Satan comes to give his two cents:

> And the chief of the spirits, Mastema, came and he said, "O Lord, Creator, leave some of them before me, and let them obey my voice. And let them do everything which I tell them, because if some of them are not left for me, I will not be able to exercise the authority of my will among the children of men because they are (intended) to corrupt and lead astray before my judgment because the evil of the sons of men is great." And he said, "Let a tenth of them remain before him, but let nine parts go down into the place of judgment." And he told one of us to teach Noah all of their healing because he knew that they would not walk uprightly and would not strive righteously. And we acted in accord with all of his words. All of the evil ones, who were cruel, we bound in the place of judgment, but a tenth of them we let remain so that they might be subject to Satan upon the earth. (*Jubilees* 10:7–11)

Satan, also called Mastema, gets a turn to talk to God too! He argues, according to *Jubilees*, that he will need at least some of these spirits. A few of them will have to help him, otherwise how will he do his job? Without spirits how would he be able to exercise his authority over humans? Satan asks God, and God listens to him. A tenth of the spirits are set aside, they are spared.

In the Old Testament, we saw the portrayal of Satan as a public prosecutor: someone who would prove whether people were righteous or not. Satan does not tempt people to sin, but keeps a close eye on you. He wants to know if you've gone astray. Satan does this on God's behalf.

Now we see a different portrayal. Satan still works on God's behalf, and definitely still needs God's permission. God even lets a tenth of the spirits live so that they can help Satan. But Satan is clearly not as innocent as he was in the Old Testament. The spirits are not there to test, they are meant to tempt and they tempt according to Satan's will. In this way, Satan has grown to be much more responsible for humanity's sins. Here, about two centuries before Jesus, we can see that the portrayal and understanding of Satan is shifting. Satan is no longer an innocent servant of God. Here he is getting his hands dirty.

Putting It All Together

We started this chapter with a short description of Satan. It was: Satan is evil. He's a rebel. He used to be an angel, but he has fallen. He didn't want to listen to God because he was prideful and so he was thrown out of heaven.

2. SATAN

Disguised as a snake he tempted Eve and thus sin was introduced into the world. He's still around and tempts each one of us.

We didn't see many of these characteristics in the Old Testament. There, Satan is hardly a rebel and he is not very evil. We could conclude that he is an angel, because he visits heaven in Job—but that is a tenuous conclusion. He has not been banned from heaven, that is clear. We also don't really see him being responsible for sin, or that he tempts people. He might well be the snake from Genesis, but Genesis does not mention it.

But now, about two centuries before Jesus' birth, things are becoming much closer to what we are used to. Satan is an angel, one of the Watchers, and he is tempting people, though maybe not directly—he has spirits to do that for him. Satan is definitely evil and wants as many people destroyed as possible. We could conclude that Satan's true nature is slowly becoming clear through the centuries.

THE PATH!

The New Testament gives us a lot of new information about Satan. But we still see some traces of the "old" Satan in various passages. In fact, some parts of the New Testament are almost incomprehensible without this old view of Satan. Join me in the letter of Jude. Jude is worried about some false teachers, and urgently writes a letter to his church. He tells them that the false teachers will get what they deserve: God's judgement. To make abundantly clear what happens to people who go against God's will, Jude gives three short examples. He reminds his listeners that the Israelites, even though they were saved from Egypt, died in the desert because they were unfaithful. He then mentions the people living in Sodom and Gomorrah. They sexually desired angels and were destroyed because of that sin. And then he gives his third example:

> And the angels who did not keep their own position, but left their proper dwelling, he has kept in eternal chains in deepest darkness for the judgment of the great day. (Jude 6)

Now that we have discovered *Jubilees*, we immediately understand what Jude is referring to: angels that left their own positions. These must be those Watchers who chased after women. The Watchers were not happy with the position God gave them and rather lived among and with humans. These angels even had children together with humans. For this they were punished. Maybe they were punished because Noah begged God to do so, as *Jubilees* claims, or maybe God came to his own conclusions. Maybe these angels are the angels that Satan took with him after rebelling in heaven. I don't know any of that. What I do know is that Jude clearly refers to that strange passage in Genesis, and to how people interpreted it through the ages.

Peter's Letter

We see something very similar in a second passage in the New Testament. Anyone who has studied the letters of the New Testament can't help but conclude that Jude and 2 Peter are very similar. If a teacher had received these two letters as exam papers, they would have had a serious conversation with brothers Jude and Peter. It is not entirely clear who copied whom, but it is clear that these two letters contain the same argumentation and even sentences! You could also say that both of them copied from a third letter, which we don't have. Whatever the case, there is much the same between Jude and 2 Peter.

Now that we have reminded ourselves of the relationship between Jude and 2 Peter, we immediately want to page through 2 Peter to see what he says about the Watchers:

> For if God did not spare the angels when they sinned, but cast them into hell and committed them to chains of deepest darkness to be kept until the judgment.... (2 Peter 2:4)

Peter refers to the angels as well. But what he is saying is much less clear. Without Jude, we probably would not have known what angels he was talking about. But considering the nature of the relationship between these two letters, we can assume that these angels are the same Watchers.

Taking these two texts together, something is very clear: all of these angels are locked up. They are chained with eternal chains of darkness. They are kept in the underworld waiting for judgement day. They clearly are not roaming the earth deceiving people. These are not the evil spirits that we know from the Gospels.

2. SATAN

More Peter

Let us look at another passage from the New Testament: a famous story from the gospel of Luke. During his last night on earth, Jesus predicts that Simon Peter will betray him in the coming hours. Jesus says this with the famous words "I tell you, Peter, the cock will not crow this day, until you have denied three times that you know me" (Luke 22:34). The gospel writers thought that this narrative was so important that all four include it in their gospel.

All four of the gospels discuss a rooster, but Luke is the only one who also discusses Satan. Before Luke quotes Jesus' prediction of Peter's triple betrayal, Jesus tells Peter something else:

> Simon, Simon, listen! Satan has demanded to sift all of you like wheat, but I have prayed for you that your own faith may not fail; and you, when once you have turned back, strengthen your brothers. (Luke 22:31–32)

This is an intriguing text indeed. It is always noteworthy when one of the gospel writers includes something that the other exclude, or vice versa. And this is not just any addition. Jesus warns Simon Peter that Satan has demanded all the disciples. He wants to sift them like wheat. What does that mean?

The word that the Bible translates with "demanded" only occurs this one time in the entire Bible. That is noteworthy in itself, as it makes it harder to understand exactly what the word means. Some secular authors use it, but also very sparingly. It means "demand," but then usually in a legal context, like a prosecutor would "demand someone for punishment," which is not good English at all. We would probably say "file charges": Satan has filed charges against all of you. This makes a lot of sense from the portrayal of Satan from the Old Testament.

Remember the book of Job. Satan goes to God and asks permission to test Job: he "files charges." Here we see something similar. Satan wants to test the disciples. He wants to sift them to separate the wheat from the chaff. It is important to note that the object of the sifting is "wheat," not chaff. Wheat is always the good thing in sifting stories. Satan wants to test the disciples' faith, but the goal, just like in Job, is to vindicate the disciples.

So what does Jesus do? Does he stop Satan? No, he doesn't. He prays that Simon's faith will endure. He does not prevent Satan from testing the disciples, even though Jesus could do that. Instead he prays for a good result. He wants Simon Peter's righteousness to be proven, just like Job's was.

In this one passage we see strong echoes of the Old Testament view of Satan. There are maybe a few more, but not many. Apparently some of the authors of the Bible were still in the process of adopting the new portrayal of Satan.

SATAN

That was a long and difficult journey. We didn't go far off the path this time—following Satan in the Bible was hard enough as it is. The traces of a not-yet-evil Satan in the Old Testament are hard to imagine, especially as many people have strong opinions of the devil.

Satan and his evil spirits are regular characters in the New Testament. We are often immediately ready to decide: Satan is evil and tempts us to sin. But if we look a bit deeper we should notice that that is not what the passage itself says. We may think it, or think we know Satan's true intentions, but the Bible is often not as clear as we may think or hope.

Should we change our opinions of Satan? I wouldn't. But we do have to look carefully at what each passage in the Bible teaches, not just what we think the Bible should teach. Was Jesus tempted by Satan in the desert, or just tested to prove his righteousness? You tell me. I still have to think about it some more. Fortunately, thinking about these questions is at least as important as having an answer.

This chapter was a challenge. What we found outside the Bible was a lot closer to what we already thought of Satan. The Old Testament portrayal was the harder one. If we had the time I could show you how Christians pieced together their understanding of Satan, leading to the image of him we have today. But this is all we have time for now.

We have arrived at our destination. We have had a tiring trip. Gladly, we can leave Satan behind us—where he belongs—and we can continue to new destinations. Which route should we take next? I'm excited already, but first, a short break.

C. How We Got the Canon

Before we can talk about extrabiblical books, it might be good to decide what "biblical" means. What are the contents of the Bible? There are, after all, a few different Bibles in circulation. Protestants like me have a Bible with sixty-six books, but there are other Christians with quite a few more books in their Bibles. Besides this, even the biblical authors quote books that they seem to think are inspired or authoritative, but not all of these books are in my Bible. Don't believe me? Look at this:

> It was also about these that Enoch, in the seventh generation from Adam, prophesied, saying, "See, the Lord is coming with ten thousands of his holy ones, to execute judgment on all, and to convict everyone of all the deeds of ungodliness that they have committed in such an ungodly way, and of all the harsh things that ungodly sinners have spoken against him." (Jude 14–15)

Jude is quoting something that Enoch must have said. Where did he get that from? He copied it from a book written about four centuries earlier, *1 Enoch*:

> Behold, he will arrive with ten million of the holy ones in order to execute judgment upon all. He will destroy the wicked ones and censure all flesh on account of everything that they have done, that which the sinners and the wicked ones committed against him. (*1 Enoch* 1:9)[1]

Jude copied this passage, in Greek almost word for word, from an extrabiblical book. Not only did he copy it, he used it as the foundation for his entire argument. Jude uses *1 Enoch* almost exactly like a pastor would quote from the Bible in a sermon.

---

1. Quotations from *1 Enoch* are from Isaac, "1 (Ethiopic Apocalypse of) Enoch."

Nowadays we don't really think about which books are in the Bible or not. For us it's totally clear and very easy to verify if a book is in the Bible. The test is simple: grab a Bible, any Bible. Is the book you are looking for in that Bible? If it is, then the book is part of the Bible. If it is not, then the book is not part of the Bible. The deuterocanonical books complicate things slightly, but you see what I mean. The canon is clear to us because it's collected in one single, physical book.

Jesus Reads a Scroll

If I tell you that books only existed long after Jesus' time, you can imagine that things were much less simple when the New Testament was written. Luke tells us of one of Jesus' adventures in a synagogue (Luke 4:16–30). Jesus goes to the synagogue on Sabbath. He stands up to read, and someone passes him the scroll of Isaiah. He unrolls it and starts to read: "The spirit of the Lord is upon me . . . ." This is a famous narrative, which we don't really give much thought. But if we pause for a moment and consider it, we can make a few notes.

Jesus is passed a scroll of Isaiah, not the whole Old Testament. There must have been more scrolls in that synagogue, but which ones? Every synagogue must have had the Torah. But did they have Malachi? Did this synagogue only have thirty-nine scrolls, or did it maybe have what we would call an extrabiblical book? Did they have a copy of *Enoch*, or *Baruch*, or *Maccabees*? If they did, did they keep these scrolls in a different place? Did they have a cupboard for the Torah, a cupboard for the rest of the Old Testament, and a cupboard for extrabiblical scrolls? Luke doesn't tell us. Sadly, no one else does either. Even archeology hasn't helped us much.

A separate cupboard, like I suggest, would make it easy to know if a scroll was biblical or extrabiblical, but all evidence suggests that the idea of a "canon" was unknown to people back then. The simple idea that it might be handy to have a list of which books are part of the Bible wasn't born yet. Why would the book of the prophet Enoch, who walked with God, or of Baruch, Jeremiah's scribe, be worth less than Isaiah or Daniel's book? Why would the book of the heroes of the people, the Maccabees, be worth less than the book of Esther? In addition to this, there was no need to agree on a definitive list. If you suddenly changed your mind, you could just move the scroll.

C. How We Got the Canon

Suddenly the Book

Once the book came into being—or, as biblical scholars call it, the codex—you had to make careful decisions. By this time we are in the fourth century, and we are talking about Christians, not Jews or Jewish Christians. You couldn't just add or remove a book inside of a book, like you could when you had scrolls. Suddenly, it was essential to think very carefully what you were going to include in the Bible and what you were not.

Additionally, the desire for a single Christianity was growing as well. This desire was born from theological fights between orthodoxy and heresy: between many groups of people with very different opinions. This was a fight not only of words but of blood. Whatever eventually won became orthodox, and whatever lost got the stamp of heresy. This battle for a single orthodox faith went hand in hand with a call for a single orthodox book. This was a call that went unanswered for centuries. Even in the late Middle Ages there was still variation in which books were included in the Bible. As an example, let's take a look at how the New Testament was canonized.

The New Testament

We have a number of sources that help us discover what was part of the Bible and what wasn't. The first source is the early Christian authors. The best citations are the ones that say: "Book X belongs in the Bible." Sadly we don't have lot of those. We can also look carefully at which books authors cite from regularly, and which books rarely get cited. This gives us an idea which books the first Christian authors thought were authoritative.

Another source is the codices: the books themselves. This is much easier to research, because you just have to look which books are included in those Bibles and which are not. A third, similar source is the papyri. These are ancient documents written on a scroll of paper made from papyrus reeds. These scrolls were very expensive, so people would fill them with as much text as possible. Often we will find multiple documents on a single scroll. If we were to find a scroll with the gospel of Judas between the gospels of Mark and Luke (a made-up example), we would be able to draw some conclusions about the gospel of Judas's value in the eyes of this writer and their community. If you know that a scroll is worth the equivalent of thousands of dollars, you know that using one to write down a particular book was never done on a whim.

Using these three sources—the authors, the codices, and the papyri—we can draw up a history of the canonization of the New Testament.

Diversity at the Beginning

In the most ancient sources, the books and letters of the first Christians, we see much diversity in what belongs in the Bible—or more correctly, in what is authoritative for these Christians. We see that many of the first Christians quote extrabiblical books. These authors soon agree that the gospels. Mark, Matthew, and Luke are beyond doubt. The gospel of John takes some discussion, but not much. The thirteen letters of Paul (Romans through Philemon) are accepted quickly too. The rest of the New Testament (Hebrews through Revelation) is a different kettle of fish. No one seems to accept James, and the rest of these books are generally accepted by one or two authors, but not by others.

To make matters more complicated, Christians from the first three centuries do accept other books as authoritative: the *Shepherd of Hermas*, the *Apocalypse of Peter*, the *Letter of Barnabas*, and the *Acts of Pontius Pilate*. These are books that most of us have never heard of.

We have collections of papyri from the third and fourth centuries that could help us, but actually they just complicate matters more. None of the papyri contain 1 or 2 Timothy, while they do include books we don't have in our Bibles today: *3 Corinthians*, the *Acts of Paul*, the *Acts of John*, and the *Gospel of Peter*, to name a few. So even in the third and fourth century we have huge diversity.

The diversity of what should or should not be in the canon continued. Around 350 the first codices were created. The two oldest that we have are Sinaiticus and Vaticanus, named after the libraries where they were kept: Sinai and the Vatican. Sinaiticus has "extra" books: the *Letter of Barnabas* and the *Shepherd of Hermas*; Vaticanus is missing Timothy, Titus, Philemon, and Revelation. About fifty years later the Bezae codex was produced. This book only has the four gospels, Acts, and 3 John. Another fifty years gave us Alexandrinus, which is missing nothing by today's biblical standard, but does have *1* and *2 Clement*. From this we could conclude that almost five hundred years after the books were first written, theologians had still not reached an agreement. The earliest codex that we have containing the twenty-seven books (and only those books) of the New Testament dates from the ninth century.

C. How We Got the Canon
Don't Worry

I have purposely only given you one side of this story. I gave this side a lot of emphasis because many Christians feel like the Bible fell straight from heaven containing sixty-six books. In fact, the opposite is true. Christians wrestled with the contents of the Bible for centuries. These books have been weighed. They have stood the test of time. In the end, these sixty-six have emerged as authoritative.

The first Christians had a number of rules or guidelines that they used to decide on a book. Firstly, the book needed to be attributed to an apostle, or someone who knew Jesus personally. That is why Hebrews was such a difficult decision: we don't know the author. Secondly, the theology of the book needed to fit with the theology of the already accepted books. This made the letters of James, Peter, and Jude controversial, as they place more emphasis on the law than Paul does.

Eventually, after centuries, having weighed and discussed everything, having prayed and having been led by God, the church agreed on the contents of the New Testament: the twenty-seven books we know today. As we look at extrabiblical books, it is good to keep this process in the back of your mind. For us the difference between biblical and extrabiblical is very large. This was not the case for the authors of the Bible, or for Christians far into the Middle Ages. It wouldn't have taken much for Revelation to be left out of the New Testament, or for our Bible to have ended with the *Shepherd of Hermas* instead. But that's not how things turned out.

3. The Messiah

Sometimes we get the feeling that all the Jews in the time of Jesus were waiting for the Messiah to drop from heaven. We seem to think that the Israelites met up at the synagogue every day to ask: "Have you seen him yet?" And then they would go home disappointed, only to meet the next day again. I'm exaggerating slightly, of course. But the point is that in thinking this, we are confused by the fact that so few people recognized who Jesus was, and we are bewildered by their confusion when he claims to be the Messiah. If we look at the narratives in the Bible more closely, though, we see that things are very different to what we usually assume. There were expectations about the Messiah, but they were diverse, varied, and often very different to what Jesus had in mind.

Let's explore the Messiah in the gospels. Our voyage of discovery is best started in the New Testament. This voyage will be different to the previous ones, because we will be spending more time in the New Testament. Messianism is such an important and intriguing topic that we hardly have to leave the usual paths. Even my brother Paul wouldn't feel the need to find a more exciting route . . . at least, not immediately.

To get us warmed up for our eventual detour, then, we will take a trip through the New Testament, exploring all four gospels to see what we can discover about the Messiah. What did people in Jesus' days expect? Ultimately, we want to know how the Messiah is described in the New Testament. Then, we will compare that with what is in the Old Testament. I can already tell you that there are differences, and that those differences help explain why Jesus was so special.

Let's start in Mark.

3. THE MESSIAH

MARK

Mark might be the second book of the New Testament, but we are very sure that it is the oldest gospel. This is easy to check. Both Matthew and Luke copy parts of Mark in their gospels: literally, word for word. So we know that Matthew and Luke used Mark's gospel when they wrote theirs. Luke and Matthew both added more than enough to make their gospels worthwhile additions to Mark, though—don't worry. Exactly those things that Matthew and Luke added are what makes their gospels so special. But it does also show us is that the gospel of Mark had to have been around when Matthew and Luke started writing.[1]

Jesus Is Tried

In Mark, when Jesus is tried in the night, several people give false witness about him. They say some very strange and contradictory things. After that, the high priest stands up and asks Jesus to reply, but Jesus seems unwilling to cooperate:

> But he was silent and did not answer. Again the high priest asked him, "Are you the Messiah, the Son of the Blessed One?" Jesus said, "I am; and 'you will see the Son of Man seated at the right hand of the Power,' and 'coming with the clouds of heaven.'" (Mark 14:61–62)

The high priest asks Jesus if he is the Messiah, the Son of God. If you look closely he asks two questions, because who ever said that being the Messiah is the same as being the Son of God? We often simply assume that they are because the only Messiah we know is Jesus, who is the Son of God. But, in fact, here we see that "Son of God" is just a characteristic of the Messiah, which is applied to Jesus at the end of his earthly life.

---

1. Now you might be thinking, "Why couldn't Mark have copied Matthew or Luke?" That's very simple to answer. There are small differences between the pieces that are in Matthew, Luke, and Mark. Sometimes a word is different or the word is in another tense. This means that one of the three changed something when copying it. Sometimes we see that Matthew and Mark are the same, while Luke is different. Sometimes we see that Luke and Mark are the same, while Matthew is different. We hardly ever see that Luke and Matthew are the same, while Mark is different. This means that Luke and Matthew couldn't have seen each other's books, but that they must have seen Mark. It is good to note that both Luke and Matthew copied from another book as well, one that Mark did not use. We don't have this book, but we call it Q.

Now, it could be that the high priest means nothing special with "Son of God." In the Bible kings are often called sons of God (2 Samuel 7:14; Psalm 2:7, 89:26–27), but Jesus does not leave this open to interpretation. He immediately says "I am" and quotes Scripture to ensure that the audience know he is not any old king. He will sit at God's right hand (a quote from Psalm 110:1) and he will come again as the son of humanity (a quote from Daniel 7:13). The high priest probably didn't understand what Jesus was saying at all, but after Jesus' death and resurrection, with the benefit of hindsight, we understand what he meant.

Jesus Asks the Disciples

Jesus' trial is not the first time that the gospel of Mark discusses the Messiah. Earlier on, we read this story:

> Jesus went on with his disciples to the villages of Caesarea Philippi; and on the way he asked his disciples, "Who do people say that I am?" And they answered him, "John the Baptist; and others, Elijah; and still others, one of the prophets." He asked them, "But who do you say that I am?" Peter answered him, "You are the Messiah." (Mark 8:27–29)

Just before this exchange happens, Jesus had healed a blind man (Mark 8:22–26). That is a good introduction to this part of the gospel. After a story about literal, physical blindness, Mark tells this story of metaphorical, spiritual blindness. The disciples cannot see who Jesus really is. Just as Jesus made the blind man able to see, so will he cure the disciples' blindness.

To help his disciples, Jesus asks them something that at first looks like a silly question: "Who do the people say that I am?" You can imagine the disciples thinking very hard. As soon as one thinks they know an answer, they shout out: "John the Baptist!" Others join in. "Elijah!" "A prophet?" We can't know if the disciples shared these ideas, or were just saying what they heard others say. But when Jesus asks them who *they* think he is, one of the disciples knows the right answer. "You are the Messiah," says Peter. Strangely enough, Mark doesn't tell us what that means. Apparently just the title was enough at that moment. But for us it is not enough. We're looking for information, because we want to know what people back then were expecting.

Peter's answer doesn't help us much, but the earlier, incorrect answers from the disciples do. John the Baptist, Elijah, and a prophet all have things

3. The Messiah

in common. In fact, they are all three pretty much the same answer. They are all prophets. Clearly, what people were expecting was a prophet. Maybe they were expecting the return of an old prophet, maybe they were expecting a new one—but they were definitely expecting a prophet.

Earlier in our analysis of Mark, we found "Messiah" and "Son of God." Now we have seen "prophet." Sadly, this is all Mark can teach us about messianic expectations in the time of Jesus. If we want to know more, we have to look elsewhere. Our next stop is Luke.

LUKE

In Mark, we started with the end of Jesus' life. In Luke, let's start at the beginning. Luke tells us how Joseph and Mary took Jesus to the temple (Luke 2:22). They wanted him to be declared clean and they wanted to bring a sacrifice to the Lord in thanks (Luke 2:23–24). Joseph, Mary, and Jesus are not the only three people in the temple, naturally. Just as they arrive they run into Simeon:

> Now there was a man in Jerusalem whose name was Simeon; this man was righteous and devout, looking forward to the consolation of Israel, and the Holy Spirit rested on him. It had been revealed to him by the Holy Spirit that he would not see death before he had seen the Lord's Messiah. (Luke 2:25–26)

Here we discover that Simeon is waiting for the Messiah. He is also looking forward to the consolation of Israel. These two things are obviously related. Simeon expects the Messiah to bring consolation to Israel.

Consolation is an important concept here. The word, which literally means "comfort," is a religious expectation, not a political one. If Luke had said "liberation," then we could conclude that Simeon's expectations had something to do with the Jewish people being ruled by the Romans. When you are oppressed, liberation solves the direct problem, whereas consolation helps you to deal with it. Often—and we will look at this shortly—we do see that the Jews were looking for liberation. But Simeon is looking for something that we know Jesus will bring: consolation for the oppressed, the weak, and the sick.

If we look for this word in the rest of Luke, we will only find it in two other places. We see consolation in the sermon on the mount, where the rich have already received their consolation (Luke 6:24). Similarly, in the parable of the rich man and Lazarus, the rich man is suffering in the underworld but Lazarus finds consolation (Luke 16:24). In both cases consolation seems to be associated with the afterlife. It is not necessarily about life here on earth, but about the promise of a better life after death. This is very much a religious expectation: they expect a Messiah who will save people from sorrow, from sin; not someone who will save them from the oppressive Romans.

Busy in the Temple

Apparently, it is busy in the temple on the day Simeon meets Jesus. Luke also tells us about a woman. Her name is Anna, and she is a prophet. Besides that, she is apparently very old, ancient even (Luke 2:36–37). The Greek is ambiguous here, but she has either been a widow for eighty-four years (e.g., KJV, NKJV) or she is eighty-four years old (e.g., NRSV, NIV). It doesn't really matter that much to us here. In an age when you were lucky to reach forty, she was well into her eighties—maybe even one hundred and four. What does matter to us is that Anna was a very devout woman. Despite her considerable age she was in the temple day and night. There she prays and fasts almost without stopping. While she is praying, she hears what is happening with Simeon, and she comes to see the Messiah too:

> At that moment she came, and began to praise God and to speak about the child to all who were looking for the redemption of Jerusalem. (Luke 2:38)

Anna is also awaiting redemption, not liberation—just like Simeon. Anna is not interested in those Romans. She awaits something spiritual and religious.

Jerusalem is the holy city, and as such it is a symbol of Judaism. Anna and Simeon, both regular temple visitors, expect a religious Messiah who will bring them religious redemption and consolation. Maybe they don't expect the far-going redemption that Jesus brought, but they are expecting something similar. Mark gave us the characteristics "Son of God" and "prophet," and now thanks to this narrative at the beginning of Luke we can add "religious liberator" to our list of New Testament messianic expectations.

3. The Messiah

Jesus and the Politician

As we reach the end of Jesus' earthly life in Luke, we see that Luke generally tells us the same things that Mark does. What we read earlier, about the Messiah, the Son of God, and the son of humanity, is all in Luke too. What we skipped in Mark was the trial before Pilate. Luke's retelling of that trial is more informative for our search than Mark's:

> Then the assembly rose as a body and brought Jesus before Pilate. They began to accuse him, saying, "We found this man perverting our nation, forbidding us to pay taxes to the emperor, and saying that he himself is the Messiah, a king." Then Pilate asked him, "Are you the king of the Jews?" He answered, "You say so." Then Pilate said to the chief priests and the crowds, "I find no basis for an accusation against this man." (Luke 24:1–4)

Jesus is on trial before Pilate. The high priests want to get rid of Jesus so they have accused him of doing three things: perverting the nation, forbidding people to pay taxes, and saying that he is a messianic king. Pilate is only interested in the third accusation. The first one is very vague, and the second one is just untrue—maybe Pilate knew that. He wants to know if Jesus is a king. So he asks him, "Are you the king of the Jews?"

Jesus answers Pilate with a strange turn of phrase: "You say so." In English this is a vague answer. It feels a bit like a politician avoiding a question, or someone who is humble affirming a statement. In the language back then this was neither political nor humble. "You say so" means something like: "Yes! Well done coming to that conclusion all by yourself." (Look at Judas and Jesus in Matthew 26:25, it is much clearer there.) Jesus *is* the king of the Jews.

We know that he means something very different to what Pilate, the priests, and the people thought. We are, however, not looking for what Jesus meant with the answer, but what people expected from a Messiah. Here we have a very simple answer: a king who will stand opposite the Roman governor. Pilate, as you may have noticed, sees no danger in Jesus' kingship. He doesn't find Jesus guilty of anything. But about twenty verses later, he proclaims him guilty anyway because he is too afraid to do otherwise.

Extreme Walking

John the Baptist Has Questions Too

King is not the only messianic expectation that we can find in Luke. Before Jesus meets Pilate, we read about Jesus and John the Baptist. John was the person who baptized Jesus at the beginning of his ministry. This was a special occasion that showed how unique Jesus was. Luke tells us the short version (Luke 3:21–22), Matthew the longer one (Matthew 3:13–17). Both tell us that the Holy Spirit came down in the form of a dove, and that there was a voice from heaven proclaiming Jesus to be the Son of God.

John the Baptist must know a lot about Jesus and his identity, but a while later, when he is in prison (see Matthew 11:2) he is having some doubts. He hears of Jesus' miracles, and decides to ask Jesus for clarification:

> So John summoned two of his disciples and sent them to the Lord to ask, "Are you the one who is to come, or are we to wait for another?" When the men had come to him, they said, "John the Baptist has sent us to you to ask, 'Are you the one who is to come, or are we to wait for another?'" (Luke 7:18b–20)

That's quite strange, don't you think? John baptized Jesus, he saw the dove and heard the voice. At the baptism he said he was not even worthy to baptize Jesus. John knows that Jesus is pretty special, but he still sends his disciples to ask Jesus whether he is the one who was to come.

Why does John ask something that he should already know? The best answer is that he has started to doubt. Apparently, he expects something from the Messiah that he hasn't seen Jesus do yet. I imagine that what John is missing is related to his situation. Thanks to the Romans he is in prison, and he clearly expects Jesus to bring liberation: for him in prison, and for the people under the oppression of the Romans. John expects a literal, political liberator. Maybe this fits nicely together with the expectation of a king, as we saw at Jesus' trial, but that is not necessarily the same thing. This we can add to our list of expectations for the Messiah: "Son of God," "prophet," "religious liberator," "king," and "political liberator."

Joseph of Arimathea

The last part of Luke that we want to discover is all the way at the end. Jesus has been crucified. Around noon it grows dark, and the curtain in the temple is torn. Jesus has spoken his last words. The Roman centurion has been converted, the crowd has gone home, and Jesus' followers stand at

3. THE MESSIAH

a distance. They do not know what to do—except for one follower named Joseph:

> Now there was a good and righteous man named Joseph, who, though a member of the council, had not agreed to their plan and action. He came from the Jewish town of Arimathea, and he was waiting expectantly for the kingdom of God. This man went to Pilate and asked for the body of Jesus. Then he took it down, wrapped it in a linen cloth, and laid it in a rock-hewn tomb where no one had ever been laid. (Luke 23:50–53)

Joseph wants to bury Jesus. Very admirable of course, but we are more interested in the description of him Luke gives us. We read that he is from Arimathea and that he eagerly awaits the kingdom of God. This is another expectation from the time of Jesus. It may resemble the expectation of a king, as I will readily admit, but I think there is a small difference. The kingdom of God is ruled by God, this means that the Messiah is not the king. Joseph does not expect the "kingdom of the Messiah," he expects a new kingdom where God is the king. I imagine that this refers to the kingdom of God that will follow the second coming of the Messiah. In fact, you could say that Joseph of Arimathea awaits the same thing Christians await: the eternal kingdom of peace. That is something quite different to an earthly kingdom where the Jews are free from Roman oppression.

That marks the end of our walk through Luke. Our next (short) stop is Matthew, and then we can move on to John.

MATTHEW

We have already discussed most of the messianic narratives in Matthew, because they are either in Mark or Luke. There is a lot of overlap between these three gospels. Still, one important story remains that is unique to Matthew: the journey of the wise people from the East.

Jesus was to be born in Bethlehem. A few magicians, often called "wise men," arrive in Bethlehem out of the East (Matthew 2:2). They have seen a star and they know that stars don't appear for any old birth. "Where is the newborn king of the Jews?" they ask (Matthew 2:2a). In other words, they are looking for a king. I will admit that these people are not Jews, so we cannot use their expectations to tell us more about what Jews in those days expected. But that doesn't really matter in this case, because we have already seen "king" elsewhere and it is already on our list.

The current "king of the Jews," Herod, almost has a heart attack when he hears about their search. As we all know, when the average king gets a fright or is in a bad mood, everyone around the king shares in his misery. Herod is, as far as that is concerned, very average (see Matthew 2:3). He quickly calls for his wise people—his scribes and chief priests—and asks them where the Messiah was to be born. Clearly, he very quickly makes a link between king and Messiah. He is not the only one. The scribes know their Scripture, and cite a passage from Micah 5 in their answer:

> They told him, "In Bethlehem of Judea; for so it has been written by the prophet: 'And you, Bethlehem, in the land of Judah, are by no means least among the rulers of Judah; for from you shall come a ruler who is to shepherd my people Israel.'" (Matthew 2:5–6)

This is neither the time nor the place to examine how they quote the Bible, but I can advise you look up this quotation in Micah 5:1. There is quite a difference between the two. What we are interested in is that these scribes quote the prophet Micah, and say that a ruler will come from Bethlehem who will guide Israel. While Herod and the magicians are interested in a king, what they quote is a passage about a ruler; a ruler who will "shepherd" Israel. This is quite different to a king who will free the people from the Romans and different to a king that will begin an eternal kingdom of peace.

The magicians continue their journey and go to Bethlehem. They are still looking for that king, and when they finally see him, they kneel down before him (Matthew 2:11). They pay him homage, which to me sounds like a religious act. They worship Jesus, which is something that you might do for a king, too, but only when that king is considered divine in some way, which most ancient kings were considered to be.

This was the only narrative in Matthew that could add to our composite image of what people back then expected. The only gospel remaining is John, let's move on to there.

JOHN

The forth and final gospel is very different to the other three. Matthew, Mark, and Luke all resemble each other closely, but John is a completely different story. It is much more theological, and more philosophical. In John, you are much more likely to hear the underlying theological reasoning than

3. The Messiah

a straightforward description of the events. Keep that in the back of your mind as we read on.

The first place that we run into an expectation of who Jesus could be is in the story of Nicodemus (John 3:1–10). Nicodemus is an important, scholarly man. He is a Pharisee, but he is also a member of the Sanhedrin, the highest tribunal council of the Jews. Clearly, Nicodemus is a VIP.

There is some bad blood between the Jewish leaders and Jesus, but nevertheless Nicodemus wants to talk to Jesus. So, he goes to Jesus at night, when no one will see him:

> He came to Jesus by night and said to him, "Rabbi, we know that you are a teacher who has come from God; for no one can do these signs that you do apart from the presence of God." (John 3:2)

Nicodemus sees and recognizes the signs that Jesus gives. This proves to him that Jesus must be on God's side—someone could only do what Jesus does through God. So he wants to talk to this special person, but he does not say that Jesus is a prophet. He doesn't say that Jesus is the Messiah, and he says nothing of redemption or liberation. Instead, he calls Jesus a teacher who has come from God. Could that be an expectation that people had at that time? That there would come a teacher? Let's see if anything else in John can confirm this theory.

Jesus At the Well

Just one chapter later, Jesus arrives in Samaria and stops at a well. There he meets a woman, and they have a conversation. Jesus seems to know a lot about the woman's life, and eventually the penny drops. She says to him "Sir, I see that you are a prophet" (John 4:19).

That the woman at the well recognizes Jesus as a prophet is not strange, because many others have done that. This woman is not Jewish, though. That makes a difference. The woman does not stop there, and continues:

> "Our ancestors worshiped on this mountain, but you say that the place where people must worship is in Jerusalem." Jesus said to her, "Woman, believe me, the hour is coming when you will worship the Father neither on this mountain nor in Jerusalem. . . . But the hour is coming, and is now here, when the true worshipers will worship the Father in spirit and truth . . . ." The woman said to him, "I know that Messiah is coming" (who is called Christ). "When he

comes, he will proclaim all things to us." Jesus said to her, "I am he, the one who is speaking to you." (John 4:20–21, 23, 25–26)

The background to this discussion is complicated, and could fill scores of books. The short version for impatient people is this: after Solomon's death Israel was split into the North kingdom and the South kingdom. The northerners were quickly attacked and taken over by the Assyrians. The Assyrians did not deport many people—in fact, many Assyrians stayed in the North kingdom. The two peoples integrated, and thus the Samaritans were born. Centuries later, after the southerners had also been taken over, the Samaritans built their own temple on Mount Gerizim. The southerlings, the "real" Jews, did not recognize this "false" temple, and rumors depicting the Samaritan religion as dodgy began to circulate. Some even spread rumors that they sacrificed children. Years later, in Jesus' day, this Samaritan Judaism had become a religion in its own right, with theology, scripture, dogmas, a holy mountain, and so on.

As you can imagine, Israel and Samaria started to butt heads over which mountain (and thus which temple) was the real one: Zion or Gerizim. The woman at the well starts discussing the mountains, but Jesus answers that it does not really matter where you worship God. He says that you only need to be in spirit and truth. We will look at spirits in a later chapter, but what Jesus is essentially saying is that place is not important. Instead, the important thing is what is inside you (spirit) and who you worship (truth). He says that a time is coming—in fact that the time is already here—when you can forget about these places.

I can see the woman thinking. She is trying to understand what this prophet is explaining. Places will no longer matter when a certain time has come, and that that time is now. She makes a logical leap and says: "You mean it won't matter because the Messiah has come . . . right?" This makes Jesus a happy man, because she knows who he really is. He is the Messiah, the one who will reveal everything, the one who will explain everything.

This is a different type of Messiah than what we had already run into. Our list read: "Son of God," "prophet," "religious liberator," "king," "political liberator," "bringer of the heavenly kingdom," and "ruler who will shepherd." In John, we see that Nicodemus awaits a teacher of some sort, and this Samaritan woman also expects someone who will explain everything. In other words, the Messiah they are looking for is a prophet who is also a teacher; I would say a divine teacher.

3. The Messiah

We will not find any other expectation of the Messiah in the gospels. Thank goodness, because this is already quite a list of characteristics! Now we are ready to compare this extensive list with the books that were written before Jesus was born. That should be a rewarding journey, because if we can't find the same information, descriptions, or names in older books, it means they must be unique to Jesus. We won't be stepping off the biblical path for a little while, because there is still so much to explore here! But first, we need a break. In this break I'll give you a brief introduction to the books between the Old and New Testaments: the deuterocanonical books.

D. The Deuterocanonical Books

In an earlier chapter, we saw how the contents of the New Testament came to be. As you can probably imagine, there was a similar process for the Old Testament. Up to the nineteenth century, scholars assumed that the contents of the Old Testament were set by the year 100 CE. But we have found quite a bit of evidence that the discussion remained heated all the way into the third century. To make matters worse, two different religions claimed this book as Scripture, and both were dealing with canonizing its contents at the same time. Just to make this process a little more complex, there was one last complicating factor: language.

The Old Testament, for the most part, was written in Hebrew. Unfortunately, many if not most Jews at the time didn't actually speak or understand Hebrew. Some probably spoke Aramaic, which resembles Hebrew, but most spoke Greek. Their Scripture (i.e., the Old Testament) had to be available in Greek, otherwise no one would understand it. Fortunately, the Bible was available in Greek, a translation that had grown piecemeal through the centuries. This translation reached its final form around 200 BCE.

Myth

The Greek translation of the Old Testament is called the Septuagint. This is derived from the Latin word for "seventy." When we refer to the Septuagint we often use LXX, which is seventy in roman numerals. You can see that seventy is an important number when we talk about this Greek translation.

The story goes—and this story is not history but myth—that the Egyptian king Ptolemy II wanted a copy of the Hebrew Scriptures in his library

D. The Deuterocanonical Books

in Alexandria. So, he called six wise men from each of the twelve tribes of Israel. This gave him seventy-two men in total. He locked all seventy-two of them up in solitary confinement and gave them a simple task: "translate the Bible into Greek." A miracle happened, because every single translation was identical.

This is a great story, but the more likely truth is that through the centuries the books were translated by various people. They were also variously edited. For most books we have older versions, so we can trace how the translation was fixed and improved. If you compare the books themselves, there is quite a bit of variation in the way language is used. Grammar and vocabulary change, meaning both that various people translated the books, but also that books were translated at different times. There is one kernel of truth to this myth, though: the Old Testament in Greek began in Alexandria.

The New Testament Prefers the Septuagint

This Septuagint was the Bible that Matthew, Mark, Paul, and the other authors of the New Testament generally read and used. How could we possibly know that? If we look at their quotes, they generally are the same as what is in the Greek, and not at all like what is in Hebrew.

A good example of this is 1 Peter. In the first chapter Peter quotes Isaiah. While Peter does quote something that resembles Isaiah in our Bibles, it is not entirely correct. Compare his quote to the text from Isaiah below:

> All flesh is like grass and all its glory like the flower of grass. The grass withers, and the flower falls, but the word of the Lord endures forever. (1 Peter 1:24–25a)

> All people are grass, their constancy is like the flower of the field. **The grass withers, the flower fades, when the breath of the LORD blows upon it; surely the people are grass.** The grass withers, the flower fades; but the word of our God will stand forever. (Isaiah 40:6b–8)

Comparing what Peter writes down to what he can look up in Isaiah, it seems as if Peter skipped a bit. I printed the bit that's missing in bold. The sentence about the breath of the Lord on the people is totally gone. That gives us two options: (1) Peter thought "Oh, that bit is unimportant, let me skip it," or (2) Peter quotes from a source that also skipped that bit.

A short search in the Septuagint shows us that it is mostly likely option 2. Compare this translation of Isaiah from the Septuagint with Peter's quote:

> All flesh is grass, and all the glory of humanity is like a flower of grass; the grass is withered, and the flower falls off, but the word of our God remains forever. (Isaiah 40:6–8)[1]

Peter literally copies this Greek translation. The translations printed above are slightly different, but the Greek is not. Because Peter copies from the Septuagint, he too skips that bit I printed in bold. If we were to do this with all the quotations in the New Testament—and people have—we would see that almost all quotes resemble the Septuagint much more than they do the Hebrew. This leads us to conclude that the authors of the New Testament must have used this translation as their Scripture.

If you think about it, it is very logical that they used the Greek Bible. We all read the Bible in our native language. The United Bible Societies work tirelessly to make Bibles available in new languages each year. Why wouldn't the Greek-speaking Jews and Christian converts read Scripture in their own language?

Two Old Testaments

We could agree that it was useful having a Greek translation of the Old Testament for the people who didn't speak Hebrew. It gets a bit more confusing when the actual contents of the Greek translation are different to the Hebrew. The Septuagint contains the thirty-nine books that we have in our Old Testament, but also several more. These books were probably never written in Hebrew, but from the oral tradition recorded straight into Greek. They must have had some authoritative status among the Jews, and thus also among the first Christians.

In other words, in Jesus' day you had two Scriptures. There was the Hebrew Scripture with thirty-nine books, and the Greek Scripture with a few more. Confusing, I know. And to top it all off, a couple of centuries later Greek started to become less fashionable. Most of the Christians no longer spoke Greek, so they needed a translation in Latin. It was much easier to translate from Greek to Latin than from Hebrew to Latin (and most Christians probably only knew of the Greek translation), so Jerome

---

1. Brannan et al., eds., *The Lexham English Septuagint*.

D. The Deuterocanonical Books

created a Latin translation from the Septuagint. This translation, the Vulgate, automatically contained the extra books.

This means that these books were always part of the Old Testament (either in Greek or Latin) that Christians read. The idea that these books might not be an original part of the Old Testament only really became evident during the Reformation. Fifty years earlier, Erasmus had arranged an Old Testament based on the Hebrew Scripture. It immediately became clear that the Greek or Latin Old Testament, which the church had been using through the ages, was different to the original Hebrew one. This meant that during the Reformation questions were raised about the validity of these "later" books, which we call the deuterocanonical books.

The struggle during the Reformation is why Catholic Bibles generally include these extra books, while Protestant ones—following the Reformers—do not. They are not Catholic books, but ancient Jewish books. While they may not be inspired in exactly the same way the Hebrew books were, they do give us a better understanding of the variety and theological depth of Judaism.

4. The Messiah Again

It is time to discover the Messiah's roots in the Old Testament. Earlier we saw that there was a lot of variety in what people expected from the Messiah in the New Testament. We saw "Son of God," "prophet," "religious liberator," "king," "political liberator," "bringer of the heavenly kingdom," "ruler who will shepherd," and "divine teacher." Now we are going to try to find these same titles in the Old Testament, starting with "king."

A KING

We want to start as close to the beginning of Old Testament as possible, and that means we begin with Genesis. Some people claim that there might be a very subtle reference to the Messiah in the blessing/curse that God proclaimed after the first humans sinned (Genesis 3:15). I think that the first real reference to the Messiah is all the way at the end of Genesis. When Jacob is about to die, he calls his twelve sons together. He talks to each one in turn and blesses him. He blesses Reuben, Simeon, and Levi. Then it's Judah's turn to be blessed:

> Judah, your brothers shall praise you; your hand shall be on the neck of your enemies; your father's sons shall bow down before you. Judah is a lion's whelp; from the prey, my son, you have gone up. He crouches down, he stretches out like a lion, like a lioness—who dares rouse him up? The scepter shall not depart from Judah, nor the ruler's staff from between his feet, until tribute comes to him; and the obedience of the peoples is his. Binding his foal to the vine and his donkey's colt to the choice vine, he washes his garments in wine and his robe in the blood of grapes; his eyes are darker than wine, and his teeth whiter than milk. (Genesis 49:8–12)

4. The Messiah Again

There is so much depth and intrigue in this blessing that hundreds of books have been written on it! The gist is not very complicated: Judah will be an excellent king. His enemies and the Israelites will bow before him. He will be as strong as a lion—so strong, in fact, that people will be afraid of him. He will have a scepter, which all kings have, and a ruler's staff. And then it gets very interesting for us. Judah will have that staff "until tribute comes to him" (Genesis 49:10). This clause is notoriously hard to translate. If you look in other translations you might see "Until Shiloh comes" (NKJV) or "until he to whom it belongs shall come" (NIV). This last one is very clearly a messianic interpretation.

Looking in other ancient translations gives us an idea how those translators understood the Hebrew. The Septuagint translates this as "until the one laid away may come to him, and he is the expectation of nations." This translation is another messianic interpretation. Other ancient versions, including some Hebrew manuscripts, read "until he comes to whom it [the staff] belongs." This too is a messianic interpretation. Therefore, while the Hebrew might be unclear, ancient readers clearly understood this as a messianic passage.

Judah will keep his staff until someone who deserves it more comes along. This will be someone to whom all the nations will be obedient. It appears that there is an expectation of a king who is even better than excellent. There will be a king greater than the lion, Judah: a king who will rule all nations. He will be a king associated with opulence.

That's right—opulence. Think about it. What kind of person ties his donkey to the best vine? Before you know it, all the grapes will have been eaten. Only two types of people tie donkeys to their choice vine: someone who is not very smart or someone who is so rich that a few lost grapes don't matter. This king is, I think, the second type. He washes his clothing in wine, which again means he is either a silly person or a very rich person. The coming king will be very wealthy and will live in opulence. He looks good too: dark eyes, white teeth. In this passage we see an expectation of a king similar to Judah, but even better, richer, and more powerful.

Balaam

Moving onwards through the Old Testament we arrive in Numbers. I have to admit that Numbers is not my favorite book in the Bible. It is often quite monotonous. But, hidden between the pages of statistics you can find the wonderful story of Balaam. We have already read a part of this narrative, when we discussed Satan earlier. If you haven't read the whole story yet, please do! Start in Numbers 22:2.

At the end of the narrative Balaam gives an oracle, or a prophecy. First, he launches into an extensive introduction, explaining that his words come straight from God (quite necessary in his case), and then he gets to business:

> "I see him, but not now; I behold him, but not near—a star shall come out of Jacob, and a scepter shall rise out of Israel; it shall crush the borderlands of Moab, and the territory of all the Shethites. Edom will become a possession, Seir a possession of its enemies, while Israel does valiantly. One out of Jacob shall rule, and destroy the survivors of Ir." (Numbers 24:17-19)

Balaam sees a star and a scepter. You don't have to be a great biblical scholar to realize that a star is the sign of a king. We already saw that in Matthew, when the magicians from the East followed the star to Bethlehem. It also shouldn't surprise anyone that a scepter can be associated with a king. This means that Balaam foretells a king in Israel's future, just like Jacob did earlier.

You could rightly ask whether Balaam refers to the Messiah or just to an earthly king in the future, for example king David. Some people think this oracle is about the Messiah. I disagree. In Judah's blessing we saw references to a king who would rule all nations, and a king more powerful than Judah. All of that is missing here. Without a hint of universal kingship, I doubt that this passage refers to the Messiah.

David and the Temple

Moving onwards in our search for kingly Messiahs, we run into David (this whole narrative is from 2 Samuel 7:1-16). One day David wakes up in his palace. He looks around and thinks, "I live in this awesome palace. God, on the other hand, is still camping out in a tent. That's not fair at all! I'm going to build a palace for God."

This is not just about being fair. It was incomprehensible for people back then not to have a temple in their capital city. People imagined the temple to be the umbilical cord of the world. A country without a temple was not connected to heaven, which meant that your country was not

4. The Messiah Again

under divine blessing or protection. In fact, your country was not even part of the universe.[1] David needs to solve this as soon as possible.

David calls his personal prophet Nathan and tells him about his plan. Nathan hears all of it, and replies, "Go ahead. Put all of these plans into action. God is with you in this." David hears this, thinks "Great!" and draws up plans for a temple. But that night Nathan receives a vision. God is not entirely on board with David's plan. Nathan receives a message for David.

"David," says God, "have you totally lost your mind? What do you mean you are going to build me a house? Who told you that I even want a house? Haven't I been living in that tent ever since we left Egypt? In all those years have I ever asked for a house?"

"It was me," continues God, "that turned you from a shepherd into a king. I have always taken care of you. I destroyed your enemies. I gave you a great name. I gave Israel a land of their own. I gave you peace, rest from your enemies.... You know what? I am going to build you a house, and not the other way around!"

God, of course, doesn't mean a literal house. He is not going to build a nice summer palace for David on the ocean. Instead, he is going to give David a dynasty: a whole list of kings all called "son of David." God says:

> When your days are fulfilled and you lie down with your ancestors, I will raise up your offspring after you, who shall come forth from your body, and I will establish his kingdom. He shall build a house for my name, and I will establish the throne of his kingdom forever. I will be a father to him, and he shall be a son to me. When he commits iniquity, I will punish him with a rod such as mortals use, with blows inflicted by human beings. But I will not take my steadfast love from him, as I took it from Saul, whom I put away from before you. Your house and your kingdom shall be made sure forever before me; your throne shall be established forever. (2 Samuel 7:12–16)

David will receive a stable kingship. If we're honest, I think this is because David probably had good intentions when he decided to build God a house. David's son is going to be king, and that son will be allowed to build a temple for God. In exchange God will take care of him, his children, his grandchildren, his great-grandchildren, and so on, forever. David's kingly dynasty will endure for all eternity.

---

1. If you are interested in this topic, my friend and colleague Jean-Claude Verrecchia wrote a very readable book on temples, sanctuaries and, of course, cosmic navels, called *God of No Fixed Address*.

This wonderful blessing for David contains a messianic promise, or at least the hint of one. Admittedly, an eternal kingdom need not literally endure forever. Most schoolchildren will tell you that the classes go on for literally forever, but they don't. This blessing could just mean "a very long dynasty," but reading backwards from the New Testament we know better. This promise is about more than David's kingdom.

Psalms and Shepherds

Staying with David and his kingship, let's look at the Psalms. In the book's second Psalm or song, the Psalmist (the author of a Psalm) writes from God's perspective. We get to hear what the Psalmist imagines is God's side of the story. They tell us God's words:

> He said to me, "You are my son; today I have begotten you. Ask of me, and I will make the nations your heritage, and the ends of the earth your possession. You shall break them with a rod of iron, and dash them in pieces like a potter's vessel." (Psalm 2:7b–9)

In 2 Samuel God already promised that the Davidic kings would be his sons. In this Psalm the same blessing is quite clear. If you look at the rest of the words that the Psalmist puts in God's mouth, though, you should notice that it is more universal than just David's kingdom. Once again, the kingdom contains all nations. It is a kingdom of the whole world. We saw that in Judah's blessing, and we see it here again. A universal kingdom of all nations. A single kingdom led by *the* Son of God.

To get to the point, people expected a king. This would be a king with a worldwide kingdom, containing all nations. It would be a king who is the son of God, ruling an eternal kingdom. You might think that this job description is more than enough for a messianic king, but it isn't. This king does more than just rule: he shepherds as well.

Ezekiel also tells us of a king who shepherds his people. He is the last prophet that we will look at for a kingly Messiah. Ezekiel has some critique about the current rulers of Israel. Speaking on God's behalf, he pronounces judgement over these shepherds who did not tend their flock properly (Ezekiel 34:2–8). Switching to the future, a promise is given:

> I will set up over them one shepherd, my servant David, and he shall feed them: he shall feed them and be their shepherd. (Ezekiel 34:23)

4. The Messiah Again

Ezekiel prophesies that there will be a new and better shepherd. God will set a shepherd to watch over Israel, and this shepherd will be... David. This is a bit confusing, to say the least. By the time of Ezekiel, David has been dead for ages. The Israelites have been captured, and Ezekiel lives in Babylon. I would not expect David to still be able to rule! But still, he is expected. Biblical scholars sometimes call this "David Redivivus," which is Latin for "David alive again." This term refers to the hope that there would be a new David, or maybe a revived David, who would be king again.

Reading backwards from the New Testament, this David is what the gospel writers would call "the Son of David." Without the New Testament, this passage is difficult to understand. In a later chapter Ezekiel once again prophesies about the new David:

> Then they shall be my people, and I will be their God. My servant David shall be king over them; and they shall all have one shepherd. They shall follow my ordinances and be careful to observe my statutes. They shall live in the land that I gave to my servant Jacob, in which your ancestors lived; they and their children and their children's children shall live there forever; and my servant David shall be their prince forever. I will make a covenant of peace with them; it shall be an everlasting covenant with them; and I will bless them and multiply them, and will set my sanctuary among them forevermore. (Ezekiel 37:23b–26)

The first passage I quoted didn't clearly show that this new David would be a Messiah figure. It shouldn't be breaking news that Israel will get a new king. Read the Old Testament: they have hundreds of kings. But here we see something special. The Israelites will follow God, and they will live in their land forever. David will be their prince, forever. This is an expectation of an eternal kingdom. A shepherd will rule this kingdom: the new David.

A King, in Conclusion

What have we learned in our research into the term "king"? We had quite a list of messianic expectations from the New Testament. If we look at the passages from the Old Testament that we read, we can check a number of boxes. "Son of God" that one was very clear. "King" was not a problem either. Seeing that this king will rule an eternal kingdom, we can tick off "bringer of the heavenly kingdom" as well. In all of these promises of future kingdoms, the Israelites were not subject to other rulers. This means that we don't have to worry about "political liberator." And, finally, Ezekiel showed as a future ruler who was also a "shepherd," just like David.

So, what are we still missing? Just three: "Prophet," "religious liberator," and "divine teacher." In other words, we have found political expectations, but we are still looking for religious expectations. Let's see if we can find some.

PROPHET AND PRIEST

Finding expectations of a religious Messiah in the Old Testament is much harder than finding expectations of a royal Messiah. You can't open the Old Testament without falling over a king, and terms like "son of David" or even "son of Jesse" are quite common. Priests and prophets, on the other hand, are much rarer. As we say, though, seek and you shall find. In Deuteronomy 16–18 there is a long list of rules, policies, and protocols for judges, kings, priests, and prophets. Halfway through chapter 18, Moses starts to talk about the prophets:

> The LORD your God will raise up for you a prophet like me from among your own people; you shall heed such a prophet. This is what you requested of the LORD your God at Horeb on the day of the assembly when you said: "If I hear the voice of the LORD my God any more, or ever again see this great fire, I will die." Then the LORD replied to me: "They are right in what they have said. I will raise up for them a prophet like you from among their own people; I will put my words in the mouth of the prophet, who shall speak to them everything that I command. Anyone who does not heed the words that the prophet shall speak in my name, I myself will hold accountable. But any prophet who speaks in the name of other gods, or who presumes to speak in my name a word that I have not commanded the prophet to speak—that prophet shall die." You may say to yourself, "How can we recognize a word that the LORD has not spoken?" If a prophet speaks in the name of the LORD but the thing does not take place or prove true, it is a word that the LORD has not spoken. The prophet has spoken it presumptuously; do not be frightened by it. (Deuteronomy 18:15–19)

This passage is a promise about the coming of a prophet that resembles Moses. This prophet will speak on God's behalf. When the Israelites saw God's power on Mount Sinai, they concluded that God was too mighty and

4. The Messiah Again

too holy to be seen or heard (Exodus 20:19; Deuteronomy 5:23–27). That's why God needs to appoint prophets to pass on his words.

But is this prophet in Deuteronomy a messianic prophet? If we are honest, it doesn't appear so. Yes, I know that if we read back from the New Testament this could be seen to refer to such a prophet. Many people in the time of Jesus expected a single prophet (John 1:19–21; 6:14; 7:40), and some New Testament authors certainly read this passage like that (Acts 3:22; 7:37). The job description of this prophet is quite a normal one, however. In fact, all the prophets through the Old Testament fulfill this position.

On the other hand, the rest of this chapter suggests that this is not a single prophet, but many prophets through the ages. The context of this passage is one where Moses warns the Israelites to stay away from divination and magic. The Israelites should not use occult methods to divine God's will. Instead, they should listen to the prophet that God will raise up. It would be quite hard for them to listen to the great Prophet, meaning the Messiah, as they would all be long dead before he came around. For them, this would sound like a terrible solution. They would have to wait thousands of years for answers, and would all turn to divination anyway! The prophet is meant to replace divination, in their lifetimes. "The prophet" that they should listen to is whichever prophet speaks on God's behalf in their own time.

Following this passage there are quite a few prophets in the Old Testament, but there are very few predictions about future prophets. In fact, there is only one, in Malachi. This prophet's name is Elijah.

The Prophet Elijah

One prediction in Malachi still plays an especially large role in the Jewish religion. At many celebrations and religious settings, a chair is kept free. This is not for any fashionably late guest, but for a single, special guest: Elijah, the greatest prophet, who was taken up into heaven (2 Kings 2:1–12). This tradition is based on a specific prophecy in Malachi:

> Lo, I will send you the prophet Elijah before the great and terrible day of the LORD comes. He will turn the hearts of parents to their children and the hearts of children to their parents, so that I will not come and strike the land with a curse. (Malachi 4:5–6)

Elijah is coming soon! Or rather, before God definitively intervenes in this world, Elijah will come back. He will remove the generation gaps, making parents and children grow closer together. Elijah will prepare people for the eternal kingdom.

With this passage in the back of our minds, suddenly the conversation between John the Baptist and the priests in John 1:19–22 becomes much more clear. "Who are you?" ask the priests. "Well, I am definitely not the Messiah," answers John. This is not really a direct answer to their question. I can imagine that the priests would get a little bit irritated by this. They continue their questioning, and Malachi 4 is in the back of their minds.

"Who are you then? Elijah, we suppose."

"Not him either."

The priests are really agitated now. Who else could this John be? Suddenly a penny drops. Maybe he is that prophet from Deuteronomy.

"Are you the Prophet?"

"Nope."

The priests must be furious by now. John does not seem to want to cooperate at all! After a few more questions they finally get some kind of answer.

"I am the voice in the desert that shouts that the Lord's road must be straightened," says John. They will have to be satisfied with that.

This is a unique passage, because it shows us quite a few expectations in a row. John is apparently not the Messiah, the new king and (son of) David. He is not the prophet Elijah that was promised in Malachi. He is also not the prophet from Deuteronomy. The priests name all the prophesied prophets, and he is none of them.

That is all we can say about a prophet as the Messiah in the Old Testament. Just two passages that we are sure about, and neither is very extensive. A truly messianic prophet is missing from the Old Testament. Yes, there are some expectations about generic prophets, and specifically about Elijah. The disciples guess that Jesus might be Elijah, or maybe another prophet. But this expected prophet expectation is not the great religious liberator that we are looking for.

Priests

We just concluded that it is hard to find expectations of future prophets in the Old Testament. As we will see, it is even harder to find expectations of

4. The Messiah Again

coming priests. There is only one passage that describes a messianic priest. This might be unexpected, as most Christians have some idea that Jesus is a heavenly high priest and the entire book of Hebrews discusses Jesus' priesthood. The one and only time we find a messianic priest in the Old Testament is in Psalm 110. This is the entire Psalm:

> The LORD says to my lord, "Sit at my right hand until I make your enemies your footstool."
> The LORD sends out from Zion your mighty scepter. Rule in the midst of your foes. Your people will offer themselves willingly on the day you lead your forces on the holy mountains. From the womb of the morning, like dew, your youth will come to you.
> The LORD has sworn and will not change his mind, "You are a priest forever according to the order of Melchizedek."
> The Lord is at your right hand; he will shatter kings on the day of his wrath. He will execute judgment among the nations, filling them with corpses; he will shatter heads over the wide earth. He will drink from the stream by the path; therefore he will lift up his head. (Psalm 110:1–7)

Fun fact: this is the Psalm that is most often quoted in the New Testament. That's with good reason, as it is full of Messianism. The Psalm can be divided into two parts. The first two paragraphs are about a king, and the last two are about a priest. The two paragraphs discussing the king are very similar to the passages we looked at earlier, but these two paragraphs about the priest are unique.

The priest is a priest forever. That makes them a very special priest. This special priest resembles Melchizedek, who is quite the mysterious figure. We only meet him once in the Old Testament. After a great victory, Abram gives a tenth of his spoils to someone called Melchizedek (Genesis 14:17–24). This man is called a priest of God, but this is ages before Aaron becomes the first priest. Besides being a priest, Melchizedek is also the king of Salem. Is that meant to be Jerusalem? Jerusalem was still centuries away from being founded! That is all we know about this man. Have I piqued your curiosity? If so, have patience; we will look at Melchizedek in detail in a later chapter.

In this Psalm, then, we see that there is a priest and a king. The king rules all. There are no enemies left standing. The priest, likewise, will be a priest forever. It seems that this psalm looks toward a future where there is a Davidic king ruling the nations, and a mysterious Melchizedekian priest ministering to the peoples. Together they lead the Israelites.

That is the only messianic priest in the Old Testament, and the last of the prophets. That great religious liberator, which we run into all the time in the New Testament, does not appear to be based on any Old Testament prediction—at least, there is not a lot of evidence for it in the Old Testament. So where does that expectation come from? On the one hand, we could say that this is just something unique about Jesus. The human messianic expectations of the Messiah were blown away by the reality of Jesus. On the other hand, there is also a social reason that we cannot ignore. To discover what that is, we need a brief history lesson.

Imagine This

It is the year 200 BCE. Jesus has not been born. You are Jewish and you know the Hebrew Bible well. You know that people expect some kind of Messiah, and you expect one too. You know some people who expect a prophet, like Elijah, to stand up. You know others who are waiting for the new king, the son of David. You remember one Psalm that talks of a priest like Melchizedek. All of this was written in Scripture many centuries ago.

You also know that it has been quite a few lifetimes between the last book of Scripture and your life. Time was not frozen between then and now, and many things have happened. Your expectations for the Messiah are not only based on what you read in Scripture, but on the history of the last several centuries. We will have to look at this history to properly understand what was going on in Israel in the time of Jesus.

Some History Never Hurt Anyone

In ancient times and cultures, the king was a figure who stood between heaven and earth. Many cultures assumed that kings were born from the gods, or at least ordained by the gods. Some even thought that the king was one of the gods. After death, a king would generally be taken up to where the gods lived, or become one of the stars, or something else equally divine.

The Old Testament shows us that it was never God's original plan to have a king over Israel. A king was not necessary, because they did not need a figure between heaven and earth. God lived among his people. But the Israelites spent too much time looking at the peoples around them. Their cultural context was too strong, and they wanted a king—just like the other nations. Eventually, they got what they asked for.

4. The Messiah Again

The kings stuck around for a long time. Some of the kings were good, some were bad. Some were loyal to God, others were unrighteous. This lasted until Jerusalem fell. Then Israel went into exile and there were no more kings. When the temple was rebuilt, and Israelites made a life in Israel again, there still was no king. This led to the question, "Who is the ruler?"

How Do You Become a Ruler?

We generally assume that there four ways to become a ruler: title, heritage, type, and charisma. Each of these four ways shows that you are the rightful ruler of a group of people.

Title

A good title generates respect. Royalty is addressed with a specific set of titles, and leaders of countries are as well. This is a way of showing respect. Normally the ruler of a country would be a king—someone we call "majesty"—but what if there is no king? Who rules then? That would have to be someone with a good title besides "majesty." "Your Royal Baronity" or "Supreme Commander" or something like that. These are impressive titles—admittedly just made up by me. Someone with a title like that must be important and fit to rule. Just having a title like this justifies your rulership.

Heritage

If you want to rule, having the right heritage is very useful. When a king dies, his oldest child—the heir—takes the throne. Nowadays that heir can be a son or a daughter, but in biblical times it would generally have only been sons. Sometimes a true heir is missing, and you're forced to choose a bastard son, born outside of a legal marriage. Such a son would not have the right title, but would still have the right blood. Sometimes there is no son at all, and a cousin, nephew, or other relative assumes the throne. Whatever their title, they still have the right heritage. This shows that as long as you can prove some sort of familial relationship to the old king, you have some right to rule.

Type

Type is an abstract term, but an example will make it quite clear. You must know some fairy tale where the king is dead. Maybe he has been dead for years. But one day a young man will become king because, for example, he has a birthmark in the right shape on the right spot. The only right that he has to the throne is based on an arbitrary physical characteristic: in this case a birthmark. But it could be almost anything: the right hair color, a certain action (like riding a donkey into town), the right victory at the right time, anything.

We call this a "type." Basically it is an event or characteristic, from history or fiction, that makes a person recognizable as part of a certain group or generic label. In the Bible we see many types regarding Jesus: born of a virgin, from the city of Bethlehem, not accepted in his own town, and so forth. Meeting a certain requirement or performing a certain action could make people justify your claim to rule.

Charisma

The last way you can be accepted as a ruler is charisma. This is the hardest one, because you either have it or you don't. Some people can do no wrong. People like how they act, how they laugh, how they talk. If a lot of people really like you, then they are likely to want you to be their ruler.

Who Is the Rightful Ruler?

Why did I tell you all of this? Simple. At this time, 200 BCE, there is no Israelite king, but the people really would like one. There is no throne and no king sits on it. There still is a temple, though, and that place is full of priests. If you think about it, priests are a lot like kings. "Priest" is a pretty nice title. You don't just get that title. You have to come from the right family. And priests are anointed, just like kings. They have the right type.

The Israelites of the day must have thought something like this: "We don't have any kings, but those priests look a lot like kings: good titles, good heritage, good type. Very impressive. Very legitimate." In a context like that, not much needs to happen for the priests to become like kings.

About 100 BCE that is exactly what happens. It is a time of civil war, unrest, and rebellion. In these times a certain family of priests, the

4. The Messiah Again

Hasmonians, gain more and more respect. They ensure that Jerusalem is religiously liberated, and later they even help it achieve political independence. These events are so important in Israelite history that these achievements are still celebrated as a Jewish holiday: Hanukkah.

Israel was part of the Seleucid Empire in those days. This was the biggest state left over from Alexander the Great's empire. After Alexander's death the empire was split among his four generals. The Hasmonians stood up against the Seleucid occupation and liberated the people. For this, the role of high priest became a hereditary position in their family. In 104 BCE, after achieving political liberation, a Hasmonian named Aristobulus declared himself king. He was the first priest-king. Aristobulus was the great-granduncle of Herod, who was king when Jesus was born. Herod, the seventh king after Aristobulus, decided—for various political reasons—not to be both priest and king, but simply king. Nevertheless, it is clear that in the time of Jesus it was quite common to be both priest and king at the same time.

For four generations before the birth of Jesus, the high priests were also the kings. These king-priests had received this position because they had arranged political and religious freedom. When Jesus was born, the Israelites still enjoyed the religious freedom, though their political freedom had been lost to the Romans.

It is logical to assume that the reality of the last century had informed the messianic expectations of the people. The great king, the son of David, must surely bring religious freedom together with the political freedom. I don't know if this is the entire reason, though. It still seems to me that Jesus was so unique, the expectations couldn't come close, no matter what they were.

TEACHER

If you have been paying close attention, you have noticed that there is still an expectation people had of Jesus that we haven't discussed: teacher. Nicodemus and the woman at the well both expected a teacher, but we didn't find a teacher in the Old Testament.

I know, I know, I promised we were going to stay on the path this time, but we have to take one small step off it. Just out of our view there is something about a teacher. We might find our answers there.

> And God appraised their deeds, because they sought him with an undivided heart, and raised up for them a Teacher of Righteousness, in order to direct them in the path of his heart. (*Damascus Document* I, 10–11)[2]

Around 1900, archeologists found a document near Cairo. Later copies of this document were also found among the Dead Sea Scrolls, in the caves near the Dead Sea. It is called the Damascus Document, because it mentions Damascus a number of times. I'll be the first to admit that Biblical scholars are not always very imaginative when it comes to naming things.

The text discusses a lot of different topics, but it seems to be intended for a very specific community—maybe even some kind of sect. This sect appears to be under the leadership of a "Teacher of Righteousness." He is very special, and leads these people to God. The document doesn't say much about his life and ministry, but his end is very intriguing:

> Thus, all the men who entered the new covenant in the land of Damascus and turned and betrayed and departed from the well of living waters, shall not be counted in the assembly of the people, they shall not be inscribed in their lists, from the day of the gathering in . . . of the unique teacher until there arises the messiah out of Aaron and Israel. . . . And from the day of the gathering in of the unique teacher, until the end of all the men of war who turned back with the man of lies, there shall be about forty years.
> (*Damascus Document* XIX, 33b — XX, 1, 13b–15a)

This Teacher of Righteousness is associated with the Messiah for several reasons. Firstly, after his death a number of people will lose the faith. They will no longer keep to the commandments, and this will have great consequences. They will not be part of the people gathered together by the Messiah. Their names are not in the book of life.

Furthermore, there is a temporal link between the Teacher and the Messiah. When the Teacher dies, it will be forty years before the Messiah comes. The Messiah and the Teacher must therefore be different people. The Teacher prepares a way for the Messiah, and there is a strong connection between the two.

Maybe these ideas were in the minds of the woman at the well and Nicodemus. Maybe the idea of a Teacher was more common, and they expected Jesus to be this Teacher. Jesus would teach them all the commandments.

---

2. Quotations from the Damascus Document are from García Martínez and Tigchelaar, *The Dead Sea Scrolls Study Edition*.

4. THE MESSIAH AGAIN

He would be the Teacher that would live just before the Messiah would come, and would show everyone how to live righteously in order to be saved.

There we go—back on the path after a quick visit to a cave near the Dead Sea. Now, empowered with that knowledge, we can bring our messianic walk to an end.

THE MESSIAH CONCLUDED

That was quite a walk, but it was certainly worth the trip. The path led us past messianic expectations in both the New Testament and the Old, and we even took a small detour via the Dead Sea. We made a long list of messianic expectations in the New Testament: "Son of God," "prophet," "religious liberator," "king," "political liberator," "bringer of the heavenly kingdom," "ruler who will shepherd," and "divine teacher." We could find some of these expectations in Old Testament predictions, but we must still conclude that Jesus fulfilled them in unexpected ways. Often, he took predictions to their extremes. He was not *a* son of God, he was *the* Son of God; not *a* prophet, but *the* Prophet; not *a* king, but *the* King. Jesus is the ultimate realization of messianic expectations. He is the fulfillment that goes beyond anyone's wildest dreams.

E. Pseudepigraphy

It shouldn't come as a surprise that ancient cultures are different from ours. This is true on many levels. I want to discuss one specific thing, though: forgery. When we hear the word "forgery," we immediately assume something illegal is going on, but people in ancient times had a very different view. Back then, it was very common to put another person's name on a book that you had written. It also appears there was no social stigma against the practice.

Everyone knew that if you said someone famous had written the book, more people would read it. Most importantly, more people were likely to believe it and accept it. Imagine if I were to write a book, and put my name on the front like so: "The newest, greatest book by Tom de Bruin." People who don't know me would only have my wonderful powers of persuasion—assuming I am good at putting those on paper—to convince and impress them. But imagine if I were to publish it with a different name on the front: Nelson Mandela, Martin Luther King Jr., Mother Theresa. People who read that book might be great fans of Mandela, MLK, or Theresa, and are much more likely to be convinced of my message.

This used to happen in secular circles, too, but it happened more often in religious ones. Imagine if it wasn't Mandela's name on my book, but Jesus'. If people really believed the book was from Jesus, all Christians would have to accept my opinions. This is the main reason why people attributed their book to someone else. We call the phenomenon "pseudepigraphy" (from the Greek for "falsely attributed"). Try saying that ten times fast.

E. Pseudepigraphy

How and Why

In biblical times, sometimes the author would put another person's name on the cover, but sometimes that was done by the readers. You are already familiar with a few examples, though you may not realize it. Think about it for a minute: the first five books of the Old Testament are often called the books of Moses, but what evidence to we have that Moses is the author? None of these books say that Moses wrote them. At most, they say that Moses wrote down or told the people some things that he had heard from God. It's quite unlikely that Moses wrote about his own death, so we can be sure that not all of those five books were written by him. The same is true for Hebrews, Matthew, Mark, John, and the Letters of John. None of these books tell us who wrote them, but many people assume Paul, Matthew, Mark and John did, respectively. Years later, readers put the names of authors on the covers of these books, but it is possible that these are not the "real" authors. In these cases it was probably never the intention of the author to deceive people. It was just a small mistake by the first Christians.

Sometimes, though, the author does put someone else's name to a book. We have already seen it a couple of times, in the *Testament of Levi* and *1 Enoch*. In both books, the first sentences announce that they were written by these ancient heroes, but they definitely weren't. In this case, the real author is being intentionally deceptive.

As I already said, present-day people like us tend to think that this is wrong or immoral. That thought was unknown to people back then, though. Back then, you just wanted your book to be read and you wanted it to make an impact. You did all you could so that people would read it. You wrote it well, with pretty sentences, but you also made sure you gave it a good author. If we try to apply our twenty-first–century morals, laws, and contexts to the practices of people two thousand years ago, then we are the ones doing something wrong.

In the Church

Even though it was culturally accepted, pseudepigraphy got less approval inside of the Christian church. The leaders of the church never included books in the Bible that they knew were pseudepigraphical. They looked for books that were actually written by people who knew Jesus. In fact, books that they knew were pseudepigrapha were even removed from circulation.

A good example of this is 3 Corinthians. We have copies of this letter, and we know that it was not written by Paul. For a while 3 Corinthians was quite popular in the church, but one day people discovered it was pseudepigraphal. After that it fell out of favor.

It's also interesting to note that in the New Testament there is evidence that people were worried about pseudepigraphy. One example is in 2 Thessalonians, look at the following two passages:

> As to the coming of our Lord Jesus Christ and our being gathered together to him, we beg you, brothers and sisters, not to be quickly shaken in mind or alarmed, either by spirit or by word or by letter, as though from us, to the effect that the day of the Lord is already here. (2 Thessalonians 2:1–2)

> I, Paul, write this greeting with my own hand. This is the mark in every letter of mine; it is the way I write. (2 Thessalonians 3:17)

What can we make of this? The author seems worried that the Thessalonians might get a fake letter, which might cause them to panic. What makes things tricky is that many scholars assume that 2 Thessalonians itself was not written by Paul, but (probably) by one of his followers. Other scholars assume it *was* written by Paul, making it one of the oldest Christian writings. If Paul was the author, he clearly decided that what his letters need are a certificate of authenticity. That is why he writes the conclusion to his letter himself—the rest was probably written by a scribe. Just as we would sign a letter, or in olden days perhaps seal it with wax, Paul writes certain words himself. We see this more often in books that are definitely written by Paul (1 Corinthians 16:21). If 2 Thessalonians was *not* written by Paul, then it seems that the author is doing his best to make his letter look extra authentic. He doesn't just put Paul's name at the top, he "forges" Paul's signature. Paul's method of writing the last lines himself would only work for the original document, of course. It is not a very reliable certification for people who only get to see copies, like us. Paul's certification method is useless to us. Paul wasn't writing letters for all ages, sadly—he was writing to his churches.

Pseudepigraphy is part and parcel of the culture of the Bible, and an important part of understanding the Bible. We might think that this practice is strange, and it might *be* strange, but we cannot judge these practices from our point of view. Fortunately, we are now armed with a bit more knowledge about pseudepigrapha. We know that the first Christians looked

E. Pseudepigraphy

for books that were authentically written by apostles, and we know that is why they chose the twenty-seven books that we have in the New Testament.

5. The Hereafter

Earlier in this book we looked at our image of heaven. In this chapter, we will look at what often seems like the opposite: our image of hell. The eternal punishments of hell are a common theme in Christianity. Some Christians question the existence of hell, others do not, but all Christians have some image of what happens to all people after death—and to those who do not end up in heaven.

Maybe it's better to talk about the hereafter, rather than hell. What happens the moment you die? Are you judged immediately, or do you have to wait for a great judgement day? Are you just dead? Do you go to heaven if you are good and to hell if you are bad? Are you rewarded and/or punished? Maybe you await your fate in a five-star hotel!

There are very large differences between the images of the hereafter, among Christians nowadays. It should not surprise us that there have always been differences. The authors of the Bible had different ideas as well.

IMAGE OF THE HEREAFTER

One of the most famous narratives of the hereafter is a parable told by Jesus. Now, I am sure we all realize that parables are not true stories. There was never a real-life "prodigal son" or a "good samaritan." Jesus tells stories to make his message clear, and he uses images and situations that his contemporaries would understand. It became clear to me just how much of a trendsetter Jesus was when a communications expert told me how hip "storytelling" is for corporations. All the big companies, from Apple, to Google, to Airbnb, have their own "story."

5. The Hereafter

One day Jesus tells a story about a rich man and a poor beggar. The rich man is very rich and very stingy, The poor man is very poor and needy. In the middle of the story, this happens:

> The poor man died and was carried away by the angels to be with Abraham. The rich man also died and was buried. In Hades, where he was being tormented, he looked up and saw Abraham far away with Lazarus by his side. (Luke 16:22-23)

In a freak coincidence, the rich man and the poor man die at the same time. Both go to the hereafter. The poor man is in a place of comfort and luxury at Abraham's side. The rich man ends up in Hades, where he is tormented. He can see the poor man far above him, next to Abraham.

If these images of the hereafter had been unclear to the people around Jesus, he would have used very different ones. This idea of an afterlife of torture must have been known to the people around him. For someone who knows the Old Testament well, though, this should be a big surprise.

You can read the Old Testament cover to cover and hardly find any passage discussing the afterlife. As far as the Old Testament is concerned, dead is dead. To quote Ecclesiastes: "the dead know nothing; they have no more reward, and even the memory of them is lost. . . . there is no work or thought or knowledge or wisdom in Sheol, to which you are going" (Ecclesiastes 9:5b, 10b). Your body is in the grave, and you know nothing. Any reference to Sheol in the Old Testament appears to be a metaphor for being dead. There are only two possible places where we could read of an afterlife in the Old Testament. We will get to those in a moment.[1]

So even though an afterlife is unheard of in the Old Testament, Jesus tells the story of a rich man and a poor man who experience a hereafter. Unlike in the Old Testament, in this hereafter there *is* work, there *is* thought, there *is* knowledge, and there *is* wisdom. This contradiction is very intriguing.

Somewhere along the way an alternative image of the hereafter emerged, and this must be what Jesus is referring to. Can you see those answers just a little bit off the path? Can you feel your curiosity taking over? I certainly can. Every day I become more like my brother Paul. We just have to step off the path for a moment—come, join me.

---

1. If you can't wait, they are Daniel 12:2 and Isaiah 26:14-19.

Extreme Walking
RAPHAEL SHOWS ENOCH SHEOL

> From there I traveled to another place. And he showed me to the west a great and high mountain of hard rock. And there were four hollow places in it, deep and very smooth. Three of them were dark and one, illuminated; and a fountain of water was in the midst of it. And I said, "How smooth are these hollows and altogether deep and dark to view." Then Raphael answered, one of the holy angels who was with me, and said to me, "These hollow places (are intended) that the spirits of the souls of the dead might be gathered into them. For this very (purpose) they were created, (that) here the souls of all the sons of men should be gathered. And behold, these are the pits for the place of their confinement. Thus they were made until the day (on) which they will be judged, and until the time of the day of the end of the great judgment, which will be exacted from them."[2] (*1 Enoch* 22:1–4)

This is a piece of *1 Enoch*—probably the oldest extrabiblical book that we have. We can easily date it to the third century BCE, and parts of it are much, much older. This means that we might be looking at the oldest Jewish description of the hereafter outside of the Bible. It also makes *1 Enoch* a good place to start looking for that alternative image of the hereafter.

Just like the other books we have looked at, *1 Enoch* was not really written by Enoch. It has 107 chapters, which makes it longer than most biblical books. The reason it's so long is because it is actually five books stuck together. It started out as one, and through the ages four other books got added. The passage above is from the *Book of the Watchers*, the oldest part. These "Watchers" are the same fallen angels that we talked about earlier.

The books tells us that Enoch needs to bring a message to the Watchers. He does so, and they ask him to relay a message to God in return. Enoch delivers that message too, and then he receives a tour of the heavens and earth. During this tour he sees a large mountain, which is where the dead live. We will discuss what he sees in a moment, but first let's look at Enoch.

---

2. Quotes from *1 Enoch* are from Nickelsburg, *Commentary 1*.

5. The Hereafter

Who Is Enoch?

Enoch is a unique person in the Bible. In the list of Adam's descendants, Enoch breaks the pattern (Genesis 5:24). For every single descendent Genesis tells us the same thing:

> When <name> had lived <number> years, he became the father of <child>. <Name> lived after the birth of <child> <number> years, and had other sons and daughters. Thus all the days of <name> were <number>; and he died.

We get the exact same phrasing for the six names following Adam. When Genesis arrives at Enoch, though, the phrasing is different. Suddenly, we read:

> When Enoch had lived sixty-five years, he became the father of Methuselah. Enoch walked with God after the birth of Methuselah three hundred years, and had other sons and daughters. (Genesis 5:21–22)

Enoch was a very special person. His relationship with God was so good that the author had to break his pattern and go out of his way to mention it. Not content to just bring it up once, he even mentions Enoch's relationship with God again in Genesis 5:24.

This is not the only exception that Genesis makes for Enoch. The last sentence of his genealogy is different as well. Instead of "and he died," we read:

> Thus all the days of Enoch were three hundred sixty-five years. Enoch walked with God; then he was no more, because God took him. (Genesis 5:23–24)

When Enoch was 365 years old, God took him. Just like Elijah, then, Enoch was taken up to heaven while he was still alive. That is quite exceptional in the Bible and outside of it. The author of Hebrews, in the New Testament, was apparently also intrigued by it (Hebrews 11:5). Even hundreds of years later Enoch's story was remarkable.

This pre-death rapture makes Enoch the perfect person to write a book. He is very holy and unique because he never died, and because he never died he could continue writing his books in heaven. These books would naturally be much better than earthly books. His name has authority, which is why a Jewish writer one day wrote a book in his name. Not too long after, four more books were stuck to that first one, and many centuries later yet another two "Books of Enoch" were written by Christians. To distinguish them from the original *Book of Enoch*, we call these books *2 Enoch* and *3 Enoch*.

Enoch and the Hereafter

Now that we can place the *Book of Enoch*, let's see what it tells us about the hereafter. At one point in *The Book of Enoch*, Enoch sees a mountain with deep caves:

> There were four hollow places in it, deep and very smooth. Three of them were dark and one, illuminated; and a fountain of water was in the midst of it.... "These hollow places (are intended) that the spirits of the souls of the dead might be gathered into them. ... These are the pits for the place of their confinement. Thus they were made until the day (on) which they will be judged." (*1 Enoch* 22:2–4)

Caves were often used to bury people, so it shouldn't be a surprise that Enoch sees the dead in these ones. Towards the end of this passage, it turns out that the caves are actually pits. They are deep, dark, and smooth—in other words, you can't easily climb out of them. Once you are in the pit, you are not getting out. We also read that there are two types of caves: light ones and dark ones. This means that a differentiation is made between the dead. Some of the dead are allowed to dwell in the illuminated cave, where there is a fountain. The rest must live in dark caves.

After this introduction to the hereafter, Enoch tells us about another strange sight. He sees one specific dead person in a cave: Abel, the second son of Adam and Eve.

> I saw the spirits of the children of the people who were dead, and their voices were reaching unto heaven until this very moment. I asked Rufael, the angel who was with me, and said to him, "This spirit, the voice of which is reaching (into heaven) like this and is making suit, whose (spirit) is it?" And he answered me, saying, "This is the spirit which had left Abel, whom Cain, his brother, had killed; it (continues to) sue him until all of (Cain's) seed is exterminated from the face of the earth, and his seed has disintegrated from among the seed of the people." (*1 Enoch* 22:5–7)

Even after all this time, Abel is not very forgiving towards his brother. Enoch would have made this trip thousands of years after Abel's death, but

5. The Hereafter

Abel will still be making a case to God until there is not a single descendant of Cain left.

It is not immediately apparent why Abel is picked out as an example in this passage, but it does show us one fundamental characteristic of the hereafter in *Enoch*: the dead can think. The dead can complain. They can file lawsuits. In other words, dead is not dead. Here, in these four caves, the dead continue to function until Judgement Day. Abel keeps making his case against Cain who—I would imagine—is also in one of these caves.

Enoch now understands all about Abel, and is intrigued by the caves themselves. He decides to get more information from Raphael:

> At that moment, I raised a question regarding him and regarding the judgment of all, "For what reason is one separated from the other?" And he replied and said to me, "These three have been made in order that the spirits of the dead might be separated. And in the manner in which the souls of the righteous are separated (by) this spring of water with light upon it." (*1 Enoch* 22:8-9)

The differentiation between the dead has now been made clear. The righteous do not coexist with the unrighteous. This is a clever move, otherwise Abel could meet Cain, which would be pretty awkward. If the righteous were all to see the people that had hurt them in life, then there would be no rest in the hereafter.

There is one cave for the righteous and there are three separate ones for the unrighteous. The righteous dead have a better cave, with light and a fountain. Both are important, as they are signs of God's presence (Psalm 36:9; John 1). All over the Old Testament we can read about how dark it is in the hereafter (Job 49:10; 38:17; Lamentations 3:6; Psalm 143:4). This is logical, because God is not there (Isaiah 38:10-20). Yet here in this one cave we see light, which suggests God is present. It's also unusual to see fountains in the hereafter. Modern science considers water to be a sign of life, and so did the Old Testament (Isaiah 49:10; 55:1; Psalm 23:2). Living water, or the water of life, is a common topic in the Bible—even if we only look at the New Testament (John 4:10-15; Revelation 7:17; 21:6).

The presence of water and light in this cave means that there is life even among the dead. God is present in the hereafter, but the living water and God's light are only available to the righteous. After describing the first cave, *1 Enoch* tells us about the other three, and about the unrighteous who dwell there:

And this has been created for sinners, when they die and are buried in the earth, and judgment has not been executed on them in their life. Here their spirits are separated for this great torment, until the great day of judgment, of scourges and tortures of the cursed forever, that there might be a recompense for their spirits. There he will bind them forever. And this has been separated for the spirits of them that make suit, who make disclosure about the destruction, when they were murdered in the days of the sinners. And this was created for the spirits of the men who will not be pious, but sinners, who were godless, and they were companions with the lawless. And their spirits will not be punished on the day of judgment, nor will they be raised from there." (1 *Enoch* 22:10–13)

Where there was just one cave for the righteous, there are three caves for the unrighteous. The first cave is the worst, reserved for the people who did terrible things and were never punished for them in life. This unfair situation is rectified and they are punished in the hereafter instead. They will be tormented until the day of judgement, after which things will only get worse: eternal scourges and torment await them. They will never be able to escape.

The next cave is a strange one, and it is not entirely clear what Enoch means here. It seems that this cave is reserved for people who have brought a case against someone else, just like Abel did earlier. Only this cave is for the unrighteous. This suggests that the second cave is for people who (for example) lived sinful lives, and were then murdered by someone else. These sinners plead their case with God. If the case is about their own murder, their lawsuits are very useful, because their murderers will also be judged.

The third cave is also for the unrighteous. The people in this cave are not punished constantly, and they will not be punished at the judgement either. Unlike the sinners in the second cave, they have already been punished for their sins during their lives. They do not need to be punished more after death.

1 Enoch shows us a number of things about the afterlife, which are very different to what we see in the Old Testament. Firstly, there is a relationship between a person's life and their death. People remember what happened to them during their lives. They are punished or rewarded according to their actions, and accepting punishment during their lifetime can prevent eternal punishment after death. A person's life and their lifestyle on earth play a role in Enoch's hereafter. In Enoch's afterlife we also see things that

5. The Hereafter

we would associate with life. The dead enjoy light. They are thirsty and can drink. They can suffer. In other words, there is another form of life after death. The dead are not in their graves, but instead actively await the day of judgement. Finally, we see that Enoch believes in a resurrection, or at least that these caves are not the final place for all the dead. Some of the righteous will remain bound in the caves forever, but others can leave after judgement. Later in *1 Enoch*, we see that the righteous enjoy a new life in Jerusalem (*1 Enoch* 24–25).

THE HEREAFTER IN THE OLD TESTAMENT

Once again, we must conclude that this passage from *1 Enoch* is quite exceptional. Almost without fail the Old Testament speaks of the grave as the final resting place of the dead. Sheol is usually meant as a metaphor: the dead know nothing and do nothing. There are, as I said earlier, only two exceptions to this.

The first is in Isaiah. Here there is a contested phrase possibly referring to the resurrection of the dead. Isaiah contains a lament about the state of Judah that ends in a song of victory (Isaiah 26). The focus here is the nation of Israel, and near the end it reads:

> Your dead shall live, their corpses shall rise. O dwellers in the dust, awake and sing for joy! For your dew is a radiant dew, and the earth will give birth to those long dead. (Isaiah 26:19)

This passage may be a promise of a future resurrection of the dead. Alternatively, it may be a metaphor for the restoration of Israel after the exile. If it does actually discuss a future resurrection of the dead, it is the oldest Old Testament passage that does. This is not an illogical assumption, though. By that time the Israelites would have known about the idea of resurrection from the Egyptian and Canaanite religions.

The second place we find a resurrection in the Old Testament is in Daniel. This passage is not at all ambiguous. It predicts a future resurrection of most of the dead:

> Many of those who sleep in the dust of the earth shall awake, some to everlasting life, and some to shame and everlasting contempt. (Daniel 12:2)

There can be no doubt that Daniel refers to a resurrection of the dead here. The dead, he says, will awake to judgement, but until that time they will sleep in the earth. This makes it unlikely that they know anything or do anything while dead.

Then, suddenly, we find a complete description of the hereafter in *1 Enoch*. This Jewish author describes a place where the dead are sorted depending on their actions in life. He talks of a place where there is torture, sickness, and accusations: a place where the dead await the final judgement.

JESUS, LAZARUS, AND THE RICH MAN

Are you ready to return to the path, back to the Bible? Let's see what we can find there using our new knowledge. When we left the path we were at the story of the rich man and Lazarus. That story is part of much longer passage. It belongs with an extensive, consecutive collection of stories that Jesus tells, and that collection starts like this:

> Then Jesus said to the disciples, "There was a rich man who had a manager, and charges were brought to him that this man was squandering his property." (Luke 16:1)

The story that follows is rather complicated. This manager—let's call him Peter—is not doing his job very well. At his yearly appraisal things went badly, and his boss is unsatisfied with his work. Peter had been warned, but there was no improvement. Now he's going to be fired. Peter does not know what to do. Back then, Israel was not a good place to be without a job. There were no social security checks that he could claim. He couldn't work on the land, because he was not strong enough. He was not willing to beg for money. Finally, he had a bright idea.

Peter's Plan

Peter calls in all the people who owe his boss money. He tells each one of them, "Quickly, don't tell anyone but we are going to reduce your debt." His clients were overjoyed—who doesn't want to be in less debt? Now Peter has arranged himself some social security: he has a group of friends who owe him substantial amounts of money. He won't have to beg after all.

The conclusion to this story is mind-boggling. Suddenly, the manager is happy with how Peter is doing his job:

> And his master commended the dishonest manager because he had acted shrewdly. (Luke 16:8a)

5. The Hereafter

This is very surprising. I would expect Peter's boss to be even more unsatisfied with him. He wasn't doing his job properly before, and now he is committing fraud. He is stealing money! If I were his boss I would be livid, but this behavior makes sense to Jesus. He concludes:

> For the children of this age are more shrewd in dealing with their own generation than are the children of light. And I tell you, make friends for yourselves by means of dishonest wealth so that when it is gone, they may welcome you into the eternal homes. (Luke 16:8b–9)

Jesus gives his disciples two lessons from this story: (1) non-Christians are smarter than Christians, and (2) they use money to make friends. This is a loose translation, but I am not taking great liberties here. At first glance, these are not the kinds of lessons I would expect to find in the Bible, but if you look at them closely they make a lot of sense.

The first lesson we can take away from the passage is this. Peter gets a visit from his boss. His boss tells him that there will be judgement: he will be fired. Peter does everything he can possibly think of to prepare himself for that judgement, and what he does is good, because when his master returns to judge him, his master is happy. Jesus' followers should do the same thing. We must admit that Peter's preparations are morally ambiguous, but this is not uncommon in the Bible. He's a bit like the man who secretly buys land because he knows there is a treasure hidden there, and is not truthful about it (Matthew 13:44). And how about the story of the poor woman and the unfair judge, where God is compared to the judge (Luke 18:1–8)? Luke wants his readership to be prepared for Jesus' coming. He wants them to do everything they can: that is very important. They need to be smart and do whatever it takes.

The second lesson is similar: use the money you have now to arrange a place to stay after the judgement. Peter knows that a judgement is coming, and he needs somewhere to rest his head. He solves his problems using his master's money: money that will be useless to him after the judgement. Jesus' followers should do the same thing. The only difference is that they will not be staying with friends, they will stay with God. Any money that they have would be useless in heaven, so they must use as much of it as they can now. With this statement, we should know that Jesus really means we ought to share the money with the poor (Matthew 12:33–34).

Money Is a God

Jesus teaches his disciples three more lessons about money, after the story about Peter and his unexpectedly merciful boss (Luke 16:10–13). The message of all three is almost exactly the same: if you can't deal with something small, how can you expect to deal with something big? The small things are the earthly possessions, while the big things deal with your identity, or who you are as a person. Concluding the lessons, Jesus says:

> "No slave can serve two masters; for a slave will either hate the one and love the other, or be devoted to the one and despise the other. You cannot serve God and wealth." (Luke 16:13)

Now things are getting serious. That last word, "wealth," is actually "Mammon" (see NKJV). This just means wealth, but it's important that Jesus gives it a proper name. Money can be an idol. It can take over God's place in someone's life. If you worship the idol Money, there will be no more space in your life for God. That means that you have two choices: either you give your money to the poor and get closer to God, or keep your money for yourself and get further from God.

The theme that Jesus is really discussing is not money, though, as many would assume. Jesus is talking about the judgement. What do you need to do in preparation for the judgement? This story and the lessons associated with it show one thing: you need to see God as your lord, not money.

Pharisees Are Listening Too

Suddenly it becomes clear that the disciples are not the only people listening to this story. There are some Pharisees there too. They have heard all of this and are not happy. They like having some spending money in their pockets. They also like to have a certain amount of status among the people. Not everyone sees that, but Jesus does. Some might think that these Pharisees are very religious and holy, but Jesus sees something totally different:

> So he said to them, "You are those who justify yourselves in the sight of others; but God knows your hearts; for what is prized by human beings is an abomination in the sight of God." (Luke 16:15)

These Pharisees might be ready for the afterlife in the eyes of others, but God knows better. They desire money and status above anything else. Jesus wants nothing to do with those desires, and he knows that God does

5. The Hereafter

not either, so he begins a new sermon. This one is meant for the ears of these Pharisees, and it has the same theme as the last sermon: the judgement.

Jesus says that the Israelites had the law and the prophets (Luke 16:16). He means that they had these writings to prepare them for God's judgement. Their Scripture should have made it clear to them how God expects them to live their lives. Sadly, this is not the case with these Pharisees. These people knew their Bibles backwards and forwards, but Jesus still has some issues with their ethics. He continues by telling them that ever since John the Baptist has been around, everyone has been invited to join the kingdom of God (Luke 16:16). Sadly, this too is not so simple. You would imagine that the Scriptures would have been enough for them to know what God's ideals are, but as far as Jesus is concerned, these Pharisees will not receive a positive outcome in the judgement. They do not follow Scripture as God intended.

Jesus Talks About the Afterlife

To illustrate his point and make everything a little bit clearer, Jesus tells another story. This story has two characters:

> "There was a rich man who was dressed in purple and fine linen and who feasted sumptuously every day. And at his gate lay a poor man named Lazarus, covered with sores, who longed to satisfy his hunger with what fell from the rich man's table; even the dogs would come and lick his sores." (Luke 16:19–21)

On the one side we have the rich man. I don't like people being nameless in stories, so I generally give them names myself. I usually take Peter, but that's not the right name for a very rich man. Let's call him Lord Reginald Abernathy III. Lord Abernathy loves money, just like these Pharisees. He has lots of money, and he makes good use of it by dressing in purple. He likes purple, but not because of the color. Purple dyes are very rare, so purple clothing is very expensive. Purple is the sign of true wealth: the color of kings (Proverbs 31:22; Mark 15:17, 20).

Lord Reginald Abernathy III also has a party every day. A party every now and then is fine. Everyone has a birthday once a year, after all. But Lord Abernathy has a feast every single day. We can all probably agree that's a bit too much. Lord Abernathy does exactly what Amos hates:

> Alas for those who lie on beds of ivory, and lounge on their couches, and eat lambs from the flock, and calves from the stall; who sing idle songs to the sound of the harp, and like David improvise on instruments of music; who drink wine from bowls, and anoint themselves with the finest oils, but are not grieved over the ruin of Joseph! (Amos 6:4–6)

I don't have to give the other, poor man in Jesus' story a name, because he already has one. This is the only place in the Bible that Jesus gives someone in a parable a name. The poor man's name is Lazarus, which means "my God helps." Lazarus is the exact opposite of Lord Abernathy. He doesn't live in a house, but lives outside the door. In fact, he *lies* outside the door. Why doesn't he stand? Presumably he is disabled in some way. On top of that, he has some horrible disease that causes his body to be covered in sores.

Poor, disabled Lazarus lies outside the door, covered in sores. He sees Lord Abernathy walk by him every day, dressed in purple. He hears the sounds of feasting every day, and he is hungry. He dreams that one day Lord Abernathy will share some of the leftovers of his parties with him, to no avail. As bad as it is, his life can also get worse, and worsen it does. Stray dogs bother him and lick his sores. He's too sick and weak to chase them away. Having read and written all that, I must admit that I'm glad I'm not Lazarus. That man has a terrible life. Lord Reginald Abernathy III, on the other hand, has a wonderful life. Too wonderful. For years, Lazarus lies at the doorstep while Reginald feasts. Lazarus suffers and Reginald lives the good life—until they both die.

Afterlife

Lazarus and Reginald die at the same time. Quite the coincidence. Lazarus is carried away by the angels, while Reginald is buried. Poor Lazarus could not even afford a burial; even that small honor was denied him. After their death, we finally come to the passage that we were so interested in. Here, we see Lazarus and Reginald in the hereafter:

> In Hades, where he was being tormented, he looked up and saw Abraham far away with Lazarus by his side. He called out, "Father Abraham, have mercy on me, and send Lazarus to dip the tip of his finger in water and cool my tongue; for I am in agony in these flames." But Abraham said, "Child, remember that during your lifetime you received your good things, and Lazarus in like

5. The Hereafter

manner evil things; but now he is comforted here, and you are in agony. Besides all this, between you and us a great chasm has been fixed, so that those who might want to pass from here to you cannot do so, and no one can cross from there to us." (Luke 16:23–26)

Now suddenly the tables have turned. On earth Lazarus used to lie on the ground and look up at Reginald, hoping for a scrap to eat. In the hereafter Reginald looks up, much further than Lazarus ever had to, and hopes for a drop of water. The tables have turned and the unrighteous person is thirsty (Isaiah 65:13). Jesus is referring to a common image of the hereafter, but one that is very different than anything in the Old Testament. Jesus describes a hereafter where the dead continue to "live." This is a hereafter very similar to the one we saw in *1 Enoch*, but it is not exactly the same.

Lazarus has got the best seat in the house. Enoch would call this the first cave. It is the place of water and light, and Abraham is also there. That is not much of a surprise: if anyone is righteous, it's Abraham. Lord Reginald Abernathy III is in the second cave, for sinners who were not judged in life. He was never punished for his behavior during his life, so in the afterlife he gets the worst place possible. He lives in a place of torture and sickness—and thirst.

Reginald might have died, but on the inside he is still the same person. We know this because he asks for Lazarus. Let's be clear here: this means he knows Lazarus's name. He knew Lazarus, and saw Lazarus every day, but he never gave him anything to eat. He knew Lazarus was suffering, but did absolutely nothing. And now, in the afterlife, he wants Lazarus to cool his tongue, just as a slave would do. In a bit, he will want Lazarus to be his messenger. You would expect Lord Abernathy to have learnt his lesson. In the punishments of the afterlife you would presume he would see that the way he lived his life was wrong. Nothing could be further from the reality. Even during his punishment he continues being the person he always was.

The Judgement

Now the theme of judgement is back on the table. Reginald could have spent his life living according to God's will, but he spent his life wearing purple, having parties, and spending money. It would not have been difficult for him to give some money to the poor. He wouldn't even have had to leave the party. Lazarus was just outside the door! Abraham answers Lord Abernathy's request by saying "Sorry. Lazarus is not coming to do your bidding." Suffering is exactly what Lord Abernathy deserves. Furthermore, just as in 1 *Enoch*, you cannot go from one place to the other. The caves are deep and slippery, and you cannot exit them. You are stuck right where you are until the final judgement.

Hearing this, Reginald begs for something else: "Can't Lazarus go warn my brothers?" (Luke 6:27–28). He is afraid that his family will end up in this place as well. Here Jesus truly returns to the theme of his message: judgement. "They have the Scriptures," replies Abraham, "that should be enough to know what to do" (Luke 6:29). Reginald disagrees with Abraham. "A dead person will bring them to repent," he answers (Luke 6:30). In other words, he knows from his own experience that the Old Testament is not enough. Knowing what you should do is not enough, you have to be *convinced* of it. And then you have to *do* it. "If they do not listen to Moses or the other prophets," Abraham answers, "why would they listen to a dead person?" (Luke 6:31). And this is the end of the story.

Jesus does not offer up any kind of conclusion. He does not give a short lesson at the end of this story, because he doesn't have to. We know what he means: be ready for the judgement and listen to Scripture. Specifically, use your money wisely. Do not turn money into an idol. Give it to the poor instead.

Jesus used a common image of the afterlife to discuss the judgement. This is much easier to do if you can "interview" people living after the judgement, which is exactly what Jesus does. Because we know what happens in the mind of the rich man after his death, we know what the stakes are.

HOME SAFE

If you look around, you will see more images of life after death in the New Testament. In Revelation 6:9–11 you can read about the dead calling to God to end the world. 1 Peter 3:19 says that Jesus preached to the dead in the underworld (see Ephesians 4:9). Preaching to the dead is only useful if the dead can actually hear. This narrative is meant to illustrate that the people who could never follow Jesus (because they died before he was born) can also be saved. These two passages are metaphors just like Luke. The dead are described as living in order to make the story easier to understand. This does not necessarily mean that these metaphors are truth. Think about this:

5. The Hereafter

Jesus says that we are the salt of the earth, but I am not salt, I am flesh and blood.

We can conclude that among the audience of Jesus and the New Testament there were two images of the hereafter. On the one hand we have the Old Testament view of "dead is dead." On the other hand there is the image of life after death. Jesus and the authors of the Bible used both images to bring their message to their audiences.

This, I think, was a great walk. We passed the rich man and the poor Lazarus, and we saw something interesting far off. Courageously, we stepped off the path and discovered *1 Enoch*. We learnt what some people back then thought about the underworld. Armed with knowledge and background we returned to our path and learned more about the place where we started. Now, we will continue our journey!

F. The Dead Sea Scrolls

The Dead Sea Scrolls were the greatest archeological find of the twentieth century, at least for biblical scholars. The exact details of this find are shrouded in mystery and myth, and you will often hear two different stories about how the scrolls were found. I don't know which one is true: maybe both, maybe neither.

One myth goes something like this: In the winter of 1946–1947, three Bedouins are staying in the desert around the Dead Sea. They are shepherds, and are sitting around the campfire at the end of a long day. Bored as they are, they decide to have a stone-throwing competition. In this area there are thousands of caves, so they play "Who can hit the chosen cave first?" Suddenly, Jum'a Muhammed Khalil hears something breaking in a cave, but he doesn't say anything. They continue their competition; the myth does not say who won. When Jum'a is back home, he tells his cousin Muhammed "The Wolf" edh-Dhib about what he heard. The Wolf goes to look in the cave, searching for hidden treasure and gold. Sadly, he only finds some clay pots and some rolled up skins with weird symbols on them—The Wolf could not read.

Another myth tells the story of a poor Bedouin shepherd. Just like in the Bible, this shepherd had many sheep, but loses one. He looks high and low, and finally finds the sheep in one of the thousands of caves. Next to the sheep he sees pots and some rolled-up skins, and on these skins are hundreds of little drawings in rows. "Strange" he thinks—he couldn't read either. The skins do look very old, though, and they are not heavy, so The Wolf or the poor shepherd—depending on the myth—takes one of the skins home. Eventually, he sells it to a Westerner for an unexpectedly large amount of money. Quickly, he returns to the cave to grab the other skins: more money! The whole clan then starts exploring caves, trying to find as many skins as possible.

F. The Dead Sea Scrolls

Soon they discover two things. Firstly, they get the most money for a reasonably sized piece. Secondly, they don't get a lot more for much bigger pieces. Being smart salesmen, they quickly create lots of reasonably sized pieces from the large pieces—earning a lot more money. As I wrote that sentence I could hear the sound of a thousand archeologists crying out. Such destruction! The Wolf, the shepherd, and their cousins do not search carefully for these skins, either. They grab what sells, and throw the rest aside. The archeologists cry louder!

A Puzzle

In the end scrolls were found in eleven caves. The last scrolls were found in 1964, seventeen years after the first find. Currently we have nine reasonably complete scrolls and fifty thousand fragments, most about the size of a postage stamp. We think that the fifty thousand fragments are part of about nine hundred scrolls. That's a lot of pieces of many different texts.

You need to imagine it like this: you are an avid collector of puzzles. You have nine hundred puzzles, and each one has a thousand pieces. First you throw away the edge pieces of all the puzzles—now you have nine hundred puzzles without edges. Then you randomly throw away pieces of each puzzle. For some you throw away almost nothing, for others almost everything. Now, you have nine hundred puzzles without edges that are all incomplete. To complicate things, these puzzles all look exactly the same: they are brown, with very hard-to-see, brown letters. Not the easiest puzzles at the best of times. Finally, you take these nine hundred incomplete puzzles that all look the same and you throw them together into one big container. That is what scientists had from the Dead Sea in 1964—a puzzle that was theoretically possible to sort, but that was terribly difficult. You can imagine why it took a while before scientists could publish completed versions of these scrolls: most of the real publications only came out after 1990.

What happened between 1964 and 1990 is quite funny. Because it was taking so long for scientists to piece together the Dead Sea Scrolls, people started to dream up conspiracy theories. You still hear some of these theories nowadays, like "the state of Israel forbade the publication of the Dead Sea Scrolls." Conspiracy theorists say that the Dead Sea Scrolls prove that Israel does not belong where it is now located geographically. Other conspiracy theorists claim that the scrolls prove that Christianity is not true: "the Vatican stopped publication." None of these theories have any merit.

The real reason for the delay in publication is very simple: it was extremely hard to put all those puzzles back together.

We don't exactly know how the scrolls got into the caves. Some people think that there was a monastery in the area, and these caves were once the monastery's library. Others say that when the temple in Jerusalem was destroyed, the priests hid the temple's library there for safekeeping. You also hear that there was a little town in the area, and that the inhabitants put all their books in the caves when the Romans attacked. I doubt we will ever know the real reason why the scrolls were in those caves. What we do know is that the Dead Sea Scrolls were found were a village used to be: Qumran. We know that this village traded with the rest of the region, and that it had a number of industries, like the production of clay and balsam. The town had a wall, and there is a graveyard with more than twelve hundred graves. Archeologists found men, women, and children in the graves. Qumran was a lively little town, with about fifty residents—lively meant something different in those days, apparently.

The Scrolls Themselves

The pots that the scrolls were kept in were made from Qumran clay. Most of the writings found there were on parchment (leather), but some are on papyrus (reed). We even found some writings scratched into clay, which we call ostraca. One very exciting writing was one scratched into copper: a map of mythological treasures hidden throughout Israel. Sadly, archeologists have never actually found any of these treasures.

Even the best scrolls are in terrible shape. They are worn away on the top, the bottom, and the outside. Each scroll is written in columns, so that means that we are usually missing the top and bottom of each column, as well as the first few columns. Most of the scrolls were written between 250 BCE and 50 CE, and most of them are in Aramaic or Hebrew, though a few are in Greek as well.

Fun fact: every book from the Old Testament was found among the Dead Sea Scrolls, except for Esther. Besides these books, there are also many extrabiblical texts. Quite a few books are apocalypses: the same genre as Daniel and Revelation. Besides that, there are writings which we call "re-written Bible" (that is, retellings of biblical narratives), hymnals, law books, and various theological tractates. Many of the extrabiblical books found

F. The Dead Sea Scrolls

among the Dead Sea Scrolls were new to us, but quite a few we already had—though sometimes only in a Greek translation.

The Dead Sea Scrolls have taught us a lot about Judaism in the time of Jesus. The many different versions of the Old Testament books that we found there have given us a much better understanding of how the Old Testament developed. To this day, hundreds of scholars are still working to put the puzzles back together and to translate the texts. And as anyone who has ever done a puzzle knows, the last pieces are always the hardest to place.

6. Melchizedek

My mother always wanted a doctor in the family. This would allow her to call them at any time, day or night, to discuss medical issues. Sadly, even though she has nine children, not a single one became a doctor—at least, not in the medical sense.

When I started to study theology, I discovered that she also always wanted a theologian in the family. Now, day or night, I get phone calls about theological issues. They generally go something like this:

"Oh, good Tom—you're up. Dad's asleep, but my hip hurt too much. I was reading the Bible."

My pastoral mind thinks, "Wonderful!" The son in me thinks, "Why couldn't she just read the newspaper?" It's the middle of the night, but I know that hoping for a better time is futile.

"Yes, Mom," I reply, "what do you want to know?"

"Well, Tom, I was reading about . . ." and then she tells me something that I have never heard of. She finishes with: ". . . and I don't understand what it means." That makes two of us!

As a biblical scholar, I am meant to know the Bible well, and I do. But God adds these passages specifically for my mother. I have no idea where she finds them. Somewhere, usually in the books that no one reads like Numbers, she finds a story of a toilet murder, an enamored collector of foreskins, walking skeletons, female bed warmers, and scores of similar stories. So in the middle of the night, after a long day's work, I am regularly woken up with a question like this:

"Why do you think God wanted David to kill two hundred men to collect their foreskins?"

"Well—wait, what? *Foreskins?*"

6. MELCHIZEDEK

"Yes, it says here that David wanted to get married. Saul said that he first had to collect one hundred foreskins. David got overenthusiastic and killed two hundred men for their foreskins. Why did God want that?"[1]

At times like these I am truly tested as a biblical scholar. It's like boot camp for theologians: trying to explain incredibly complicated and opaque biblical passages in the middle of the night, all the while having to whisper so as not to wake my wife. I must admit I often just make something up on the spot, and then go find a better answer at a more Christian hour.

My Mother Called About Melchizedek

One cold winter's night, I received a call from my mother about Melchizedek. Specifically, my mother wanted to know: "Who's this Melchizedek character?" That was a good question, but this time I knew the answer. This time it was no toilet murderer or foreskin collector—just a priest from Genesis. I wouldn't have to spend hours researching it the next morning, because I had already done that research for a book I wanted to write about extrabiblical writings (this book).

My mother read the passage out loud to me. It's from Hebrews 5:

> As he says also in another place, "You are a priest forever, according to the order of Melchizedek." In the days of his flesh, Jesus offered up prayers and supplications, with loud cries and tears, to the one who was able to save him from death, and he was heard because of his reverent submission. Although he was a Son, he learned obedience through what he suffered; and having been made perfect, he became the source of eternal salvation for all who obey him, having been designated by God a high priest according to the order of Melchizedek. (Hebrews 5:6–10)

This passage made my mother anxious. "And, Tom," she said, "he keeps coming up. I wasn't going to bother you about this, but every chapter is about this Melchizedek."

She's right. Melchizedek plays a very large role in Hebrews. He's not in the Bible much, but in Hebrews—and nowhere else in the New Testament—Melchizedek is mentioned nine times. So far we've been talking about me and my mother, but what would my brother do in this situation? We have caught a brief glimpse of Melchizedek, and Paul would immediately want to discover more.

1. If you want to read this story, it's in 1 Samuel 18:17–30.

Come on then. Let's go exploring.

MELCHIZEDEK IN THE OLD TESTAMENT

Melchizedek is all over Hebrews, but he isn't mentioned at all in the rest of the New Testament. You can, however, find him here and there in the Old Testament. We first run into this man in Genesis, in a passage that you might have heard before. It's the first time the Bible speaks about giving tithe to the Lord.

At this time Abraham is still Abram. Lot, his nephew, lives in Sodom, and Sodom has not yet been destroyed. A king with an unpronounceable name, Chedorlaomer, goes out to war with some of his allies (Genesis 14:1–13). This is followed by violence, murder, and people falling into tar pits. In the end Chedorlaomer and his allies beat the people they attacked. One of these people is the king of Sodom. Chedorlaomer takes all of Sodom's goods and provisions, and takes some people captive too—including Lot. Abram hears about this and decides to do something (Genesis 4:14–16). He gathers everyone who can fight, and chases after Chedorlaomer. There are exactly 318 of them. With these fighters, Abram attacks the king and his allies and beats them. He gets all the stolen goods and provisions, and frees the captives. The story continues, and we finally meet Melchizedek:

> After his return from the defeat of Chedorlaomer and the kings who were with him, the king of Sodom went out to meet him at the Valley of Shaveh (that is, the King's Valley). And King Melchizedek of Salem brought out bread and wine; he was priest of God Most High. He blessed him and said, "Blessed be Abram by God Most High, maker of heaven and earth; and blessed be God Most High, who has delivered your enemies into your hand!" (Genesis 14:17–20)

Abram was traveling back and saw two men: the king of Sodom and the king of Salem. Of course the king of Sodom is there. He wants his people and goods back. The king of Salem is a new one, though. In fact, this king is not mentioned anywhere else in the story, and neither is a place called Salem. Nevertheless, there they are, Salem and Sodom, waiting for Abram. The king of Salem is named Melchizedek, and besides being a king, he's a priest too. Not just any priest, though: he's a priest of the Most High.

Now, Melchizedek came prepared. He has a packed lunch, and they all eat together. After the meal he blesses Abram, and after receiving the

6. MELCHIZEDEK

blessing Abram gives one-tenth of everything to Melchizedek (Genesis 14:21). You can imagine that his story intrigued people through the ages. Where is this place, Salem? Salem means "peace." Is that related to the story in some way? Where did Melchizedek come from? Who's son is he? Did he have children? Where was he born? When did he die? *Did* he even die? How can he be a priest of the Most High before the tabernacle was built? He's not a descendent of Aaron, so how can he be a priest at all? This is the first time God has priests in the Bible. Where did they come from? Could Melchizedek be the great-great-great-grandfather of Aaron and Levi? And how can he bless Abraham? To bless someone you have to be "greater" than the other, and surely no one is greater than Abraham, the father of Israel!

You can imagine that these and other questions kept people occupied for a good long while. It's easy to see that the Israelites would have speculated about this mysterious figure. Let's dig into those questions, then, so we can find answers. These won't necessarily be the *right* answers, but they will tell us what some people thought about Melchizedek.

MELCHIZEDEK AT THE DEAD SEA

> But, Melchizedek will carry out the vengeance of God's judgments, and on that day he will free them from the hand of Belial and from the hand of all the spirits of his lot.[2] (11QMelchizedek II, 13)

In the caves near the Dead Sea, in the eleventh cave that they discovered, archeologists found a document about Melchizedek. The Dead Sea Scrolls didn't have any titles on them, so we gave them our own. This scroll is called 11QMelchizedek: the eleventh cave (11), in Qumran (Q), about Melchizedek. It was written at least one hundred years before Jesus, and might be quite a bit older. In this scroll Melchizedek is portrayed in a way that reminds me of Michael in Revelation 12, or even of the Messiah.

Sadly, all the Dead Sea Scrolls are only partly preserved. The best ones have only lost the outsides and the edges of the scrolls, but the worst are in hundreds of pieces. 11QMelchizedek only has one column that we can read. That is a great pity, because many questions remain after reading that small part of the scroll, but what we do have tells us a lot about Melchizedek. Read with me:

---

2. Citations from 11QMelchizedek are taken from García Martínez and Tigchelaar, *The Dead Sea Scrolls Study Edition*.

> And as for what he said: "In this year of jubilee, you shall return, each one, to his respective property," concerning it he said: "This is the manner of the release: every creditor shall release what he lent to his neighbour. He shall not coerce his neighbour or his brother, for it has been proclaimed a release for God." Its interpretation for the last days refers to the captives, who . . . and whose teachers have been hidden and kept secret, and from the inheritance of Melchizedek, for . . . and they are the inheritance of Melchizedek, who will make them return. And liberty will be proclaimed for them, to free them from the debt of all their iniquities. (11QMelchizedek II, 2–6a)

This text is not very easy to understand. Especially around the ". . ." parts, where the scroll is too decayed to read. Nevertheless, we get the gist. The author is discussing the last days, when God will judge humankind. There is a link to the year of jubilee, which is a year when debts are forgiven (Leviticus 25:13; Deuteronomy 15:2). The End of Days is similar to a year of jubilee: the only difference is in the type of debt. At the End of Days, God will forgive the debts of sin. The scroll also discusses prisoners. Elsewhere, God also promises the release of captives (Isaiah 61:1). These captives are not the people who are in prisons worldwide, but the captives of unrighteousness.

Next we have two sentences that we can't really make out. They say something about the "hidden" and "secret," and then talk about the "inheritance of Melchizedek." The inheritance of Melchizedek gets explained in the next sentence: this is a return to life, liberty from sin, and freedom from the debt of iniquity.

Now, ask yourself this: would you be surprised if I had replaced Melchizedek with Jesus in those sentences? "Jesus will free everyone from the debts of inequity": it fits perfectly. Melchizedek is clearly a Messianic figure here. Do you remember Psalm 110, which we read when we discussed Messianic expectations? It also mentioned Melchizedek:

> The LORD has sworn and will not change his mind, "You are a priest forever according to the order of Melchizedek." (Psalm 110:4)

It would seem that this Psalm inspired the author of 11QMelchizedek to interpret Melchizedek as a Messianic figure again in his own work.

6. Melchizedek

Melchizedek was, as far as the author of 11QMelchizedek is concerned, a very special person. He is not just a priest from Genesis, but is someone related to forgiveness and redemption. And his role just keeps growing:

> As is written about him in the songs of David, who said: "Elohim will stand in the assembly of God, in the midst of the gods he judges." And about him he said: "And above it, to the heights, return: God will judge the peoples." As for what he said: "How long will you judge unjustly and show partiality to the wicked? Selah." Its interpretation concerns Belial and the spirits of his lot, who ... turning aside from the commandments of God to commit evil. But, Melchizedek will carry out the vengeance of God's judgments, and on that day he will free them from the hand of Belial and from the hand of all the spirits of his lot. (11QMelchizedek II, 9c–13)

The big question here is: what does the first sentence mean? The author applies Psalm 82:1 to Melchizedek, but how does it work? Is the author calling Melchizedek "Elohim," or is he saying that he is part of the assembly of God? The first option might sound very peculiar, because you may have heard that the Hebrew word "Elohim" means "God." This is not entirely true. The Hebrew word can be translated with a number of English words. It can mean "heavenly beings," or more specifically "angels," which is how Psalm 8:5 is often translated into English (except in the NRSV). So it might not be God standing in the assembly of God, but a heavenly being: Melchizedek. Alternatively, it might be God standing in the assembly, which includes Melchizedek.

Putting aside this ambiguity, the implications stay the same either way. Melchizedek is called a heavenly being: he is not just a human priest, but is a part of God's heavenly assembly (like in Job 1:6). He sits in the midst of the "gods." He is part of the council who hear and execute God's judgement. He will attack Belial—just another name for Satan (2 Corinthians 6:5)—and his spirits. Melchizedek will free humanity from the dominion of evil.

In other words, Melchizedek is a very special person according to 11QMelchizedek. He is "Elohim," or at the very least one of the leaders of God's divine council. Melchizedek will appear in the last days and will arrange atonement between God and humanity. As one of the first to hear God's judgement, he will also be the one to execute it, and destroy the forces of darkness. After reading these passages there is no doubt that for many Melchizedek is much more than a priest from Genesis.

Extreme Walking

2 ENOCH TELLS US MORE ABOUT MELCHIZEDEK

> And this child will not perish along with those who are perishing in this generation, as I have revealed it, so that Melkisedek will be the priest to all holy priests, and I will establish him so that he will be the head of the priests of the future.[3] (2 Enoch 71:29)

In ancient times books were often attributed to famous historical figures. We discussed this earlier in the chapter entitled "Pseudepigraphy." One problem with this is that there were a limited amount of famous people, so soon enough multiple books were attributed to the same person. The more famous a person was, the more books they eventually "wrote." We have three ancient books called "Enoch"—all three by completely different authors. Ezra was the most popular as far as I know: besides his book in the Bible we have five more "Ezras" outside it. We also have four Baruchs, two Abrahams, three Adams, two Josephs, two Jacobs, and two Solomons.

We often call 2 Enoch "Slavonic Enoch," because the only copies that survived were in the Slavonic language. This book tells us about Enoch's life, about his trip through the seven heavens, and about his descendants, and especially about his son Methuselah and his great-grandson, Nir (who was Noah's younger brother). The last two chapters of 2 Enoch are all about Melchizedek. We will get to the links between Melchizedek, Methuselah, and Nir in a moment, but first we need to establish the basic story, because that in itself is already very, very strange and may be quite shocking.

Lamech, Enoch's grandson, has two sons: Noah and Nir. Lamech's father Methuselah, who lives in close connection to God, receives a vision:

> Listen, Methusalam![4] I am the LORD, the God of your father Enoch. I want you to know that the days of your life have come to an end, and the day of your rest has come close. Call Nir, the second son of your son Lamekh, born after Noe, and invest him in the garments of your consecration. And make him stand at my altar. And tell him everything that will happen in his days, for the time of the destruction of all the earth, and of every human being and of everything that lives on the earth, is drawing near. (2 Enoch 70:3b–4)

---

3. Quotes from 2 Enoch are taken from Andersen, "2 (Slavonic Apocalypse of) Enoch."

4. The names in 2 Enoch look a bit strange as these are based on the Slavonic spelling. This means that Methusaleh is called Methusalam, Lamech is called Lamekh, Noah is Noe, and Melchizedek is Melkisedek.

6. Melchizedek

The Lord tells Methuselah to call his grandson Nir. He needs to pass on his priestly garments to Nir, to ordain him before God's altar and tell him all about the future. This future is given to Methuselah in the next verses in great detail. All of humanity will become depraved, bad things will happen, and then God will send a flood. Methuselah wakes up and is quite shocked, but he does what the Lord has commanded. Nir becomes a priest, and becomes the new hero of the story.

Nir is married to Sopanim. Their story is very similar to Abraham and Sarah's. They are both very old and they never were able to have children, but just like with Abraham and Sarah, they miraculously and suddenly conceive:

> And Sopanim was in the time of her old age, and in the day of her death. She conceived in her womb, but Nir the priest had not slept with her, nor had he touched her, from the day that the LORD had appointed him to conduct the liturgy in front of the face of the people. (2 *Enoch* 71:2)

Sopanim is about to die, and then discovers that she is pregnant. The only problem is that ever since Nir became a priest, they have not been sleeping together. Sopanim is too ashamed by her unexpected pregnancy to tell anyone, including Nir, and so she decides to go into hiding. For 282 days (a little bit more than nine months) she hides. On the 282nd day, Nir suddenly remembers that he hasn't seen his wife in a while:

> And when 282 days had been completed, and the day of birth had begun to approach, and Nir remembered his wife, and he called her to himself in his house, so that he might converse with her. (2 *Enoch* 71:4)

After 282 days, Nir realizes that he misses having conversations with his wife. Sopanim must have wondered why he couldn't have waited just one more day, as this was the day of birth. Nevertheless, she goes to Nir and he sees that she is pregnant. This is a big problem given their home situation, and he, too, is very ashamed. He shouts:

> What is this that you have done, O wife? And (why) have you disgraced me in front of the face of these people? And now, depart from me, and go where you began the disgrace of your womb, so that I might not defile my hand on account of you, and sin in front of the face of the LORD. (2 *Enoch* 71:6)

Nir tells his wife to get out of the house and go to the man who got her pregnant. He does not want to be associated with her sin, especially not as a priest.

Sopanim begs for mercy: "O my lord! Behold, it is the time of my old age, and the day of my death has arrived. I do not understand how my menopause and the barrenness of my womb have been reversed" (2 *Enoch* 71:7). But Nir does not believe a word she says. She has to leave. He shouts a bit more and even threatens her with violence. Before he can get any angrier, however, Sopanim falls down dead.

She had said that it was "the day of her death," and apparently she meant that literally. Nir, standing over her body, feels rather guilty at this point. He thinks: "Could this have happened because of my word, since by word and thought a person can sin in front of the face of the LORD? Now may God have mercy upon me! I know in truth in my heart that my hand was not upon her. And so I say, 'Glory to you, O LORD, because no one among mankind knows about this deed which the LORD has done'" (2 *Enoch* 71:10–11). In a panic, he runs all the way to his brother Noah's house, and tells him everything.

If you didn't already think this plot sounded more like something from a horror movie than the Bible, what happens next should convince you. Noah, ever the pragmatist, consoles Nir: "Don't let yourself be sorrowful, Nir, my brother! For the LORD today has covered up our scandal, in that nobody from the people knows this." (2 *Enoch* 71:14). Nir doesn't have to be worried—Sopanim's death was a gift from God! Now no one would have to know that she was pregnant. Together Noah and Nir run back to the house, and they prepare Sopanim for burial. Then they go out back and dig a grave in secret.

When they return to pick up the body, though they notice something strange. There is a child sitting next to Sopanim's dead body! The child (who we assume must be Sopanim's) appears to be about three years old, and is talking. Moreover, he is praising the Lord and he has a badge of priesthood on his chest.

Noah and Nir are astounded. Together they shout out in unison: "Behold, God is renewing the priesthood from blood related to us, just as he pleases" (2 *Enoch* 71:20). They wash and dress the child in priestly garments, and then they name him . . . Melchizedek. Now you know why I have been telling you this very long and strange story. 2 *Enoch* tells us that Melchizedek is actually Noah's nephew, born to an infertile woman who

6. Melchizedek

hadn't had sex with anyone in a very long time. *A woman who had already died.* As if that wasn't enough to make him special, he was also a priest from birth, and was born as a fully developed three-year-old.

Now we can get to the part of the story that's directly relevant to our discussion. Noah and Nir fear for the child's life, so they hide him. All around them everyone seems to be growing more and more evil. Nir knows that the flood is coming, he knows that he will die, but he wonders what will happen to Melchizedek. He asks the Lord, and the Lord answers:

> Nir, the great lawlessness which has come about on the earth among the multitude which I shall not tolerate. And behold, I desire now to send out a great destruction onto the earth, and everything that stands on the earth shall perish. But, concerning the child, don't be anxious. Nir; because in a short while I shall send my archistratig,[5] Michael. And he will take the child, and put him in the paradise of Edem, in the Paradise where Adam was formerly for 7 years, having heaven open all the time up until when he sinned. And this child will not perish along with those who are perishing in this generation, as I have revealed it, so that Melkisedek will be the priest to all holy priests, and I will establish him so that he will be the head of the priests of the future. (2 *Enoch* 71:27b–29)

God still intends to destroy almost all of humanity, but he intends to make an exception for Melchizedek. Melchizedek will not join Noah in his ark. Instead, the Lord will send Michael, one of the archangels, to pick up Melchizedek and take him to Eden. Melchizedek will live where Adam and Eve lived, and from there he will reign as the head of all the priests.

God promises, and God delivers. A few days later the angel Michael appears in the middle of the night to pick up the child. Nir is confused at first (just like I was confused when my mother called at a strange hour about Melchizedek), but the archangel explains everything. Michael calms the boy, and after that he gives Nir a prophecy:

> And when the twelfth generation shall come into being, and there will be 1070 years, and there will be born in that generation a righteous man. And the LORD will tell him that he should go out to that mountain where stands the ark of Noe, your brother. And he will find there another Melkisedek, who has been living there for 7 years, hiding himself from the people who sacrifice to idols, so that they might not kill him. He will bring him out, and he will be the first priest and king in the city Salim in the style

---

5. An archistratig is similar to an archangel. It is a name for an important general.

of this Melkisedek, the originator of the priests. The years will be completed up to that time—3432—from the beginning and the creation of Adam. (*2 Enoch* 72:6)

Michael's prophecy is curious and confusing. He says that in 1070 years there will be a righteous man. I think this must be Abraham. This man will meet a Melchizedek on a mountain, but he will not be the Melchizedek from this story. The original Melchizedek will still be in Eden, but this "second" Melchizedek will be a priest and the king of Salem, just like the first Melchizedek is a priest.

The author seems to be trying to solve a problem: namely, how is it possible that Melchizedek was a priest in Abraham's time (Genesis 14:17–20) and a priest forever (Psalm 110:4)? There are two logical solutions to this problem. The first solution is that the Melchizedek in Genesis lived forever . . . but then why don't we ever see him again after Genesis 14? The other solution is that there are two different Melchizedeks. The first, heavenly Melchizedek, is the eternal priest. The second, earthly Melchizedek from Salem, is a "normal" priest. He's not a priest for all ages, but he is a priest in the order of Melchizedek.

MELCHIZEDEK IN A NUTSHELL

When we read Genesis 14, we had quite a few questions from the start. What and where is this Salem place, which means peace? Who was Melchizedek's father and who are his descendants? When did he live? How could Melchizedek be a priest before there was a tabernacle? Is he related to Aaron and Levi? Most importantly, we questioned how Melchizedek could bless Abraham. After all, who could possibly be greater than Abraham, the father of Israel?

We still don't have the answers to all of these questions. If this chapter had been a book, I could have shown you more. Even though we didn't have the time to dig deeper, though, we have already found quite a few answers. People in the time of the Bible had imagined quite a few things about Melchizedek. They also knew many more background details, which we can read in extrabiblical books. According to *2 Enoch*, Melchizedek is the son of Nir, and the nephew of Noah. Melchizedek has been a priest since his birth, and was ordained by Nir, who was ordained by Methuselah in turn. This means that Melchizedek is not a distant ancestor of the priests: he is the metaphorical father of all priests. He is greater than Abraham—at least,

6. MELCHIZEDEK

according to 11QMelchizedek, where he is a heavenly being and a part of the divine council. Melchizedek will execute God's judgement on the last day, and will make atonement between humanity and God.

If we had more space we could read Josephus, a Jewish historian, to learn more. He tells us that Melchizedek built the first temple and founded Jerusalem (i.e., Jeru-*Salem*). With his help, we could answer most of our other questions as well—but least we already have one answer. There are many conflicting answers as well, deriving from many more stories and legends.

MELCHIZEDEK IN HEBREWS

We have explored off the path, and seen some very unusual things. Now we can return to our route and revisit Hebrews with new eyes. Hebrews is a complicated New Testament book, with unique theology. It focuses on Christ, which is not unique by itself, but Hebrews discusses and interprets Christ in a very special way.

In Hebrews 5 and 6 we run into the same quotation from the Old Testament (Psalm 110) three times, each time without any explanation. Three times we read that Jesus is a high priest according to the order of Melchizedek (Hebrews 5:6, 10; 6:20). As a reader you have to ask, just like my mother did, "Who is this Melchizedek?" and "How is his priesthood different to the Old Testament priests?" Two chapters later, Hebrews finally discusses Melchizedek in a bit more detail. In the beginning this discussion is quite simple and easy to understand:

> This "King Melchizedek of Salem, priest of the Most High God, met Abraham as he was returning from defeating the kings and blessed him"; and to him Abraham apportioned "one-tenth of everything." His name, in the first place, means "king of righteousness"; next he is also king of Salem, that is, "king of peace." (Hebrews 7:1–2)

Most of these verses are direct quotes from Genesis. Melchizedek blessed Abraham, and Abraham paid him tithe. We have already read that. Hebrews only adds a little bit of its own explanation. His name means "king of righteousness"—that is new information for us, but probably not for those who can speak Hebrew. *Malki* means king, *tsedek* means righteousness. *Malki-tsedek* must mean king of righteousness. The same reasoning applies to the king of "Salem," which is just a bastardization of *shalom*, meaning peace—a different explanation than Josephus gave. So far there is nothing really unexpected or extraordinary, but that changes fast.

The story continues: "Without father, without mother, without genealogy, having neither beginning of days nor end of life, but resembling the Son of God, he remains a priest forever" (Hebrews 7:3). This verse is much more complicated than the previous ones, but with our extrabiblical experience these claims about Melchizedek are not unexpected. Melchizedek has neither father nor mother. He has no genealogy, no beginning or end. None of these claims were in Genesis, but we saw something similar in 11QMelchizedek and 2 *Enoch*. They don't say that Melchizedek is without a mother, but 2 *Enoch* does claim that he doesn't have a father. Sopanim was pregnant without having had any intercourse. In both writings, Melchizedek has no end, but lives on into eternity in heaven or in Eden.

What is happening here? Hebrews clearly refers to several famous stories about Melchizedek. We could only discuss a few extrabiblical sources, but in others Melchizedek does not have a beginning either. Hebrews is using these common mythological tales to illustrate how special Melchizedek's priesthood was. The Levites were priests because their parents were Levites. They did not earn their priesthood, they got it because they had the right parents. Melchizedek, however, didn't inherit his priesthood. He was a priest without beginning and without an end. We could put it like this: he was always already a priest.

We saw something very similar in Melchizedek's miraculous birth in 2 *Enoch*. Melchizedek was born as a three-year-old after his pregnant mother died. He was born already adorned by the mark of the priesthood and did not inherit his position from his parents. As an inhabitant of Eden, he would remain a perfect priest forever. In 11QMelchizedek, where he is a heavenly being and even resembles the Messiah, it is similarly clear that his priesthood is much greater than that of the Levitical priests.

Now we get to the important part for us. No matter how special Melchizedek is, how unique his priesthood is, how independent he is of heritage, or how infinite he is, Jesus' priesthood is equal, if not greater. Jesus is not a priest for a lifetime, or even two or five lifetimes. Jesus is not a priest because he was born to the right family. Jesus is a priest independent of heritage: the perfect priest.

That was a lot of information about Jesus in just one sentence! After that sentence, Hebrews tells us more about how great Melchizedek was, and thus how great Jesus is. Firstly, he is great because Abraham, the father of

6. Melchizedek

Israel, paid him tithes (Hebrews 7:4). The Levites collected tithes among their brothers and sisters (the rest of Israel), but Melchizedek collected tithes from outside of his family (Hebrews 7:5-6a). More importantly, Melchizedek blessed Abraham. To be clear, if you bless someone, you are "superior" to that person (Hebrews 7:6b-7). Melchizedek is therefore superior to Abraham.

Then the argument gets a little bit tricky. Hebrews says "One might even say that Levi himself, who receives tithes, paid tithes through Abraham" (Hebrews 7:9). In other words, Levi, who as a priest should normally *receive* tithes, paid tithes to Melchizedek. How, you might ask? It's simple: Levi was "still in the loins of his ancestor when Melchizedek met him" (Hebrews 7:10). When Abraham paid tithes to Melchizedek, he had his son Isaac, grandson Jacob, and great-grandson Levi in his "loins." I wouldn't take this literally. Even back then they knew that biology worked differently to that. This is just a metaphor: Abraham is the metaphorical father of every Israelite (see Matthew 3:9; John 8:29), and so when he paid tithe to Melchizedek his descendants were symbolically included in the gesture.

Now we know how extraordinary Melchizedek's priesthood is—and how special Jesus' priesthood is by association. Hebrews does not stop there, however. It continues to tell us more about the various priesthoods, and about Jesus in particular.

Priests

As far as priests are concerned, on the one side there are the Levitical priests in the Old Testament. On the other side, there is Jesus' priesthood, which seems to be something new (Hebrews 7:11). The mere fact that the Levitical priests needed to be replaced shows that they were not perfect. They were good—just not good enough.

There are clear differences between Jesus the priest and the priests before him. To start off, Jesus was not a Levite. He was born into the tribe of Judah—the tribe of kings, not of priests (Hebrews 7:14). Secondly, Jesus didn't become a priest because of his heritage. His parents were not priests (Hebrews 7:15-16). Instead, he became a priest because of the power of his "indestructible life" (Hebrews 7:16), which is stronger than death. Jesus became a priest in a totally different way to earlier priests. He is a far superior priest, but Hebrews explains that if the priesthood has changed, then the law must have also changed (Hebrews 7:12). Priests are servants of the law, and the manner of priesthood is defined by the law. If there is suddenly another type of priest, we have to assume that there is also a different law.

Let's step back for a moment and think about this. We could compare the situation to driving a car. If your car is running on empty, you stop for gas. In many countries you have a choice: petrol or diesel. There doesn't seem to be much difference: the hoses are right next to each other, and sometimes the one costs less than the other. From experience I can tell you that while there might not seem to be a big difference on the outside, there is on the inside. If you put diesel in your petrol car, you have a very bad day. Now, imagine if you fill up with diesel every day for years, and suddenly one day you have to fill up with petrol. What does that mean? If the gas you use changes, then something must have changed under the hood. You must have a different engine. It is the same with the law: if the priests are different, then the religion must have changed under the hood. There must be a different law.

Perfection

The difference between the two laws, old and new, has everything to do with perfection. Hebrews explains the difference in a terribly complicated sentence, which contrasts the old commandments with the new hope:

> There is, on the one hand, the abrogation of an earlier commandment because it was weak and ineffectual (for the law made nothing perfect); there is, on the other hand, the introduction of a better hope, through which we approach God. (Hebrews 7:18–19)

The law was ineffectual because it could not make anything perfect, and so the old commandment has been revoked and replaced with a new hope. Many people hear "perfection" and automatically think about ethical perfection. That is, they think it means that you always need to make the right choices, always have to think the right thoughts, and always need to have the right wishes. Some people say we can achieve that, if we only try hard enough. We can grow more and more perfect until we have no more un-Christian thoughts, wishes, or needs. It's a nice thought, maybe, but terribly mistaken. You might be able to stop doing un-Christian things, but you can't control what you think about. It's like the famous saying about pink elephants: never having an un-Christian thought is medically impossible. Hebrews tells us that the law—that is, keeping to a set of rules

6. MELCHIZEDEK

for living—"made nothing perfect" (Hebrews 7:19). Laws can never bring perfection.

If you try to imagine perfection and law (meaning the rules and religious system of the Old Testament) you get the following: Firstly, God has a plan for the world. If you want to be part of that plan, you need to be part of the people, or the community around the temple. You will trust in the sacrifices that the Levitical priests bring to God. If the entire community is faithful in visiting the temple and making sacrifices, God will make the community perfect. If the Israelites are perfect, all the nations will be perfected through them. We will have achieved heaven on earth.

The problem is that the reality is very different. The Israelites could never be perfect, and that was never God's plan. The first type of priests were never meant to be a permanent solution. They only pointed the way to the real perfection that Jesus brings. This perfection is achieved through a totally different system. It is not the ethical perfection that so many think of, but substituted perfection through Jesus.

Ethical perfection, as I just discussed, is perfection according to the law, through the old system. It has never been God's plan for humans to live perfect lives after Eden. That would be impossible, because then they could remove the sin from their own lives. Real perfection is substitutionary perfection. In this kind of perfection, everything in the world is according to God's plan. All the puzzle pieces are in the right spots. People are part of this plan, but it is much more than just what we do. Perfection is the ultimate goal, and God will make perfection happen through Jesus.

Once we have figured that out, Hebrews really gets interesting. We can all live according to a new priesthood that is eternal rather than temporary. This priesthood has a new law. Unlike the old law, this new law *does* bring perfection. Through this new priesthood of Jesus, we have "a better hope" (Hebrews 7:19), and can come into God's presence. We do not have to strive after unachievable perfection, but need only believe and hope for God's new world, which is coming soon. In this new world everything is perfect, according to God's will.

If that is not good news, then I don't know what is.

THAT WAS MELCHIZEDEK

At the beginning of this chapter, my mother called me up in the middle of the night to ask about Melchizedek. It turns out that she had a very good question. In the middle of Hebrews, my mother saw something that led us off the path. We went out exploring, full of questions about that unique priest Melchizedek. While looking for the answers we have seen many strange and wonderful things.

Now we know that there was quite a lot of speculation about Melchizedek—from Messiah to miraculous birth, from the destroyer of Satan to an inhabitant of Eden. Hebrews even compares Jesus to Melchizedek to show us how special he is. Jesus is a much better priest than the Levites ever were, and he brings us to something much better. Not to the impossible perfection of hard work, but to the imminent perfection of God's grace.

Just off the path we saw something incredible. Back on the path we found the gospel, as clear as it has ever been. Right in the middle of the road, in the bright of day, we learnt more about Jesus, who will come to save us and take us to God's new, perfect world.

G. Bible Translations

Every now and then a new Bible translation is published. Some people rejoice because this new translation speaks to their hearts in a way that the old ones never did. Others resent it, and prefer the words that they know so well. This is quite normal—after many years of reading you get used to "your" translation.

One of the issues we run into with Bible translations is that language changes over time. The language I speak is not the same as the language my great-grandparents spoke. For the most part this is logical. It's easy to imagine why the New King James Version replaced "concupiscence" with "evil desire" (Romans 7:8). If I had not just looked up Romans in a more modern translation, I would have had no idea what "concupiscence" even means. I doubt I am alone in this.

Some words, like concupiscence, become unfashionable. Eventually we forget what they mean. Other words start to mean something totally different with the passage of time. If you read the King James Version, you will run into the word "truth" many times (e.g., Genesis 24:27; Deuteronomy 32:4), you will usually see "truth" in the New King James in the same places. But if you look in another modern translation (NIV, NRSV), you will not see "truth" there at all. This is because language has changed. When the King James Version was translated, the word "truth" meant "faithful." So when the Greek and Hebrew words for "faithful" had to be translated in 1611, the translators used *their* word for it: "truth." Nowadays, though, no one uses "truth" for faithfulness and we just misunderstand these passages. Genesis 24:27 doesn't say that God is truth, for example: it says that God is faithful.

Problems with New Translations

Change in language is not the only trouble that we have with new translations. There is something much bigger to contend with. Let me give you an example. Remember the Lord's Prayer? How does it end? Most Christians know it by heart:

> And lead us not into temptation, but deliver us from evil: For thine is the kingdom, and the power, and the glory, for ever. Amen. (Matthew 6:13 KJV)

Christians are generally quite attached to that ending. We like the sound of those three things that should remain forever: kingdom, power, glory. Most importantly, we like to end our prayers—especially the Lord's Prayer—with "Amen." The problem is that in other more modern translations this whole sentence is missing! Here is that same verse in the New Revised Standard Version:

> And do not bring us to the time of trial, but rescue us from the evil one. (Matthew 6:13 NRSV)

"For thine is the kingdom" is totally gone . . . well, banished to a footnote. The Lord's Prayer just ends with "rescue us from the evil one." No power, no kingdom, no glory—not even an amen! You can imagine that this ruffles some feathers, and from ruffled feathers conspiracy theories are soon born.

"The Illuminati are changing the Bible!" Or, depending on the person shouting, the people changing the Bible are the Freemasons, the New World Order, the Powers of the World, a mysterious Shadow Government, the Church of Satan, or the Germans. These are all ideas that some Christians made up to rationalize the changes I just described.

Conspiracy theories are usually founded on fear, which in turn is founded on ignorance. Sadly, thousands of people add to this fear and ignorance every day with silly YouTube videos, lectures full of half-truths, and books filled with strange theories. Let me explain what is actually happening, why these changes to the Bible have happened, and why, if you really want to blame someone, you should blame a group of Germans.

G. Bible Translations
The Whole Truth

Archeologists are special people. They like to dig in the slowest way possible: with a paintbrush. In the last century and a half archeologists have been busy digging in and around Israel. For decades, people have been digging there to learn more about the history of Israel and Christianity.

They find all manner of things—and if they are very lucky they find an ancient document. In the last hundred and fifty years they have found very old parts of the Bible. This causes problems. At the same time, we have found other ancient copies of the Bible in church and monastery libraries. These also cause problems. The problem is this: the Bible that we have always used, which the King James Version was based on, and which is the final result of two millennia of faithful copyists, is often quite different to the pieces of the Bible we find in the ground or in ancient libraries.

This is potentially a big problem . . . so what do you do? You have four options: (1) you quickly destroy the piece you found, (2) you ignore the piece you found, (3) you doubt the piece you found and call it a fake, (4) you change your current Bible. Scholars chose the fourth option: change the Bible. From a scholarly perspective this is totally logical. The oldest version is, after all, the closest to the original version we will probably get. It's a bit more complicated than that, but we will get to that in a moment.

Imagine this: an archeologist finds a copy of the Lord's Prayer from the first century. This version is slightly different to the version we know and love. It would be logical to assume that the copy they found is closer to what Jesus said. "Our" Lord's Prayer has been copied ten thousand times. We all know that children's party game: you stand in a row and everyone whispers a message into their neighbor's ear. At the end of the row the message is often totally different to what you whispered at first. The Bible was passed down the same way, but then spread out over two thousand years of copying and copying. It stands to reason that one or two changes must have crept in. The whispering game might make you think that there have been lots of changes to the Bible, but generally the changes are quite minimal. More than 99 percent is exactly the same . . . but still, here and there a sentence needs changing.

Extreme Walking

Now the Complicated Version

My example was the simple version, but the reality is much more complicated. We found not just one piece, but hundreds of thousands. Archeologists often have no idea which one is "right" or older, and so don't know which one to choose. A German scholar in the nineteenth century set out to solve this once and for all. His name was Eberhart Nestle—like the chocolate. Years later, just after the Second World War, another German named Kurt Aland took over this task. Nowadays, there is a very large group of scholars doing this same research in Germany. Every few years they publish a new edition of a book with the Latin title *Novum Testamentum Graece* (The Greek New Testament). The first edition was published in 1898, and I have the twenty-eighth edition on my desk. What are these scholars doing all day? Basically, they compare all the variations of the Bible that we have and choose which one is likely to be the oldest. They tell us all about the variations in footnotes, so that we can check their choices, and these choices are based on a few simple rules.

The first rule used is *Lectio difficilior potior* (literally, "the hardest reading is the strongest"). This rule states that if you have two variants, the *least* logical one is correct. The reasoning behind this idea is simple: when you are copying a book you will fix errors. Imagine you read this text:

> Tom was playing soccer, and someone passed him the ball. It was the final minute of play. He aimed carefully and kicked the wall. GOAL!

What do you think? Perhaps it's: "Haha! A typo in a book—these people are not very smart." In your head you have already fixed "wall" so that it reads "ball." If you were copying this book, you would also fix it in your copy.

But what if the more difficult reading, "kicked the wall," was the right one? Because the writers of the Bible were not always the best at grammar, a lot of "mistakes" were fixed by copyists. Illogical sentences were made logical . . . but sometimes those illogical sentences were actually fine. That monk fifteen hundred years ago just didn't notice.

Our second rule is *Lectio brevior praeferenda* (we prefer the shorter reading). If you have two texts, the shorter one is probably the original. Humans tend to add things to texts rather than remove things from them—except, of course, if you skip over a whole long bit by mistake. This didn't

G. Bible Translations

happen very often though, because the monks were very careful—more on that soon.

One thing we do see is that many people added "Christ" after "Jesus." This is probably because they were so used to seeing the two names together. Other examples include people adding a few words to make sentences clearer. "What a man!" would change into "What a man is Peter!" You might not expect these things to cause problems, but in some cases they did. In addition to "Christ," often people would add "Son of God" behind Jesus. It was automatic. Nowadays we know that these "Son of God"s were added, so we have removed them in recent translations, but because this phrase is missing, many Christians look at contemporary translations and say that the new Bibles are removing Jesus, or trying to make him less important.

We have a few more Latin sayings, and a few more rules for tracing the Bible back to its oldest copies. I won't mention them all—just a few examples. Sometimes you have a sentence that contains the same word twice so the copyist might jump from one word to another. They might skip part of a sentence, or write the same part of the sentence twice. This could also happen with letters, especially if the word was repetitive. You might end up with something like "bananana" or "bana" instead banana. Hearing this, you might think these people copying were not very good at their job... but what if I told you that Greek was written in all caps, without spaces or punctuation? THENYOUCANIMAGINETHATSOMETIMESTHEYMADEAMISTAKE.

New Translations

Hopefully, you now see that it is perfectly logical that the text of the Bible has changed a bit over the last few centuries. Rest assured: the new text is *much* better than the old. Scholarship has brought us closer to what the authors originally wrote, and the new translations are based on that text, using language as we use it today. I would advise everyone to keep a recent translation next to their old favorites. This way you can be sure you don't misunderstand the Bible because of our changing language, or new archeological discoveries.

7. Spirits

> In the beginning God created the heavens and the earth. He created the first human and placed inside of them the seven spirits of humanity. Satan saw this and corrupted the spirits. Seven evil spirits were created. God gave humankind an eighth spirit, the mind, in order to choose between good and evil.

If we were able to listen to a two thousand-year-old sermon by one of the first Christians, we might hear something like the passage above. Spirits were a huge part of the worldview of people living then. Much larger than you would imagine. This means that early Christians had a very different view of the Holy Spirit than we often do.

I, as a modernized Westerner, find it hard to imagine a spirit. I know the stories of ghostly ghouls. I hear stories and experiences of the evil influences of demons. I know the feeling of comfort that we sometimes experience when the Holy Spirit is present, but that's about it. The New Testament is quite different to me. There are a multitude of spirits, and these spirits are very different to how we imagine them nowadays. The New Testament doesn't actually teach us this, but you can constantly see that it is in the back of the mind of the writers.

> Beloved, do not believe every spirit, but test the spirits to see whether they are from God; for many false prophets have gone out into the world. (1 John 4:1)

John says we need to test the spirits. Quite a strange warning. I would imagine that you would know pretty quickly if you had an unclean spirit or a demon. If you read the gospels, it becomes clear that demons do bad things to you. Things you would notice: being mute or blabbering senselessly,

7. Spirits

going blind, having extraordinary strength or going wild (Matthew 12:22; Mark 1:24–26; 5:3–4; Luke 8:27).

If you were to suddenly go blind, or chatter senselessly, surely you'd know that something was amiss? It would be the shortest test in the world:

"Do you have a spirit?"

"Yes."

"Okay, let's test it. Have you gone blind?"

"Yes."

"Well then it is an evil spirit."

I would not call this a difficult test. In fact, it's so simple, it's not even worth writing down. It's hard to imagine that someone would have felt the inhabitation of a spirit, suddenly were unable to talk, and then thought "Hallelujah! I have a spirit from God!" Maybe if they were overly chatty, one of their family members would have thought that, but then only sarcastically.

There must be more to this passage in 1 John than simply these demons that make you wild, sick, or blind. Unclean spirits have to be more than demons that possess you. That is interesting. According to 1 John there is a nuance in the spirits, more than you would expect from the gospels. This we will have to discuss and discover. We will need to research them. Look, there, just a little way off the path. We don't have to go far to study this. My brother Paul is already walking there; will you join us?

REUBEN'S SEVEN SPIRITS

> Seven spirits were given to humankind at creation. They are responsible for all human actions.[1] (*Testament of Reuben* 2.3)

In this book's first chapter we read the *Testament of Levi*. His brother, Reuben, has a testament too. I didn't mention this before, but at some point in time one author collected materials and wrote the testaments of all twelve of Jacob's sons, beginning with Reuben all the way up to Benjamin. One big, fat book with interrelated last words. We call this book the *Testaments of the Twelve Patriarchs*.

The *Testament of Reuben* contains Reuben's final advice to his sons— or at least that's what the book wants you to believe. The book tells you all

---

1. The quotes from the *Testaments of the Twelve Patriarchs* are from Bruin, *Great Controversy*.

about Reuben's life, especially his mishap with Bilhah, one of his father's wives (Genesis 49:4). His book mainly discusses the danger that women form for men. Women are really sexy, which is tempting, and men are simple creatures with only one thing on their minds. If they are not very careful they will make a mistake, just as Reuben did with Bilhah.

But I digress. This book tells us how sick Reuben became after his misstep. He had some ailment in his loins. This is quite appropriate considering his sin. He was in such agony that he was forced to repentance, and he begged God for forgiveness. Just as he is doing that, he received a vision from the Lord about the nature of humanity:

> And now, my children, listen to what I learnt, after my repentance, about the seven spirits.... Seven spirits were given to humankind at creation. They are responsible for all human actions. (*Testament of Reuben* 2:1a, 3)

According to Reuben's vision, humanity consists of seven spirits. God placed these spirits inside of humans at creation. Now you might already have an idea what this spirit is, but you are probably wrong. These spirits are the construction blocks of humanity.

People back then didn't know a whole lot about biology. Nowadays we tend to think of our body as a machine, but that idea was unknown two thousand years ago. They did know that we had all manner of organs, and that these organs did something. So they thought: "How can an organ do something unless it has a spirit in it? Your stomach can't just get hungry. A spirit must be responsible."

How did they reach this conclusion? The reasoning is actually quite simple. Humans need to breathe to live. Obviously, there is something in the air that we need. What is there in air? Spirits! So we need to keep breathing this air-spirit. But if you open someone up, you will only see air in his lungs. That must be the place where air-spirit is converted to blood-spirit. Your blood, which they thought worked like tides, transports the blood-spirit to your whole body. In this way the spirits in your body are fed.

Naming the Seven Spirits

In those days, everyone assumed that there were spirits inside of each person. Reuben tells us exactly which ones they were:

7. Spirits

> (1) The spirit of life, with which nature is created. (2) The spirit of sight, with which comes desire. (3) The spirit of hearing, with which teaching is given. (4) The spirit of smell, with which taste is given to inhaled air and breath. (5) The spirit of speech, with which comes knowledge. (6) The spirit of taste, with which comes eating and drinking, and with which their strength is created (in food is the foundation of strength) (7) The spirit of sexual reproduction and intercourse, with which sin enters by the love of pleasure. (*Testament of Reuben* 2:4b–8a)

Reuben describes seven spirits. The first is the spirit that God breathed into the human at creation: the spirit of life. After that we see that the spirits are similar to the senses, but they are more extensive than that. Hearing is also teaching, talking is also knowledge. The final spirit is, at least for Reuben, the most dangerous: the spirit of sexual intercourse. That spirit led Reuben to the wrong bed, which did not work out great for him.

So for Reuben, there are seven spirits in each person. We should understand this image in the following way: the spirits live in you, they are part of you, but behave independently from you. So, if you feel curious, you aren't *really* curious yourself. It's the spirit of talking that's curious. If you are hungry, it's not really you, but the spirit of taste.

It's quite similar to what we mean when we say "my stomach's rumbling." You're just hungry, but you associate it with an organ that is part of you. People back then did the same, but then with spirits instead of organs.

Evil Spirits

Besides these godly and natural spirits there are also evil ones. We know that there is evil in the world. Satan doesn't want you to be saved. That's why he poisoned God's perfect creation at the very beginning. He introduced sin into the world:

> Beliar [i.e., Satan] gave humankind seven spirits, and from these stem the works of youth. (*Testament of Reuben* 2:2)

Satan also gave humanity seven spirits; we'll see how soon. These seven spirits lead to evil deeds. Reuben calls them the works of youth, because Reuben, as a young man, slept with the wrong woman. Sexual misconduct was, especially then, seen as something young men just did.

Just a few verses further Reuben explains how Satan distributed the evil spirits. He mixed his misleading spirit with the seven spirits God gave to humanity:

> The spirit of deceit is mixed with these. (1) The spirit of fornication situated in the nature and the senses. (2) The spirit of greed in the stomach. (3) The spirit of battle situated in the liver and the gall. (4) The spirit of flattery and trickery, that through vain effort they may appear beautiful. (5) The spirit of arrogance, that they may be boastful and conceited. (6) The spirit of lying: molding words and keeping secrets from their house and family through depravity and envy. (7) The spirit of unrighteousness, with which come thefts and double-dealing, so that they may attain their heart's desire. For, unrighteousness cooperates with the other spirits by means of bribes. (*Testament of Ruben* 3:2–6)

Satan ensured that all humans have evil spirits together with the good ones. Naturally the evil spirits also number seven. These spirits are the opposites of the good spirits. As Satan's spirit, the spirit of deception, mixed with the spirits God gave humanity, evil copies of Gods spirits came into existence. They are the evil mirror image of the good spirits. The spirit of intercourse is mirrored by the spirit of fornication, the spirit of taste by the spirit of gluttony.

Humanity has a tough lot. On the one side God gave us spirits, but they don't necessarily lead us to good. On the other side, we have the evil spirits, which definitely lead us to evil. Thus, each person is drawn towards sinning. Fortunately, however, humanity can do some good. Let's see how.

Doing Good

God put seven spirits in humanity to lead each person, Satan added seven spiritual carbon copies to lead them to evil. But that is not the entire story. Later in the *Testaments of the Twelve Patriarchs*, we run into Judah's testament. There we learn how choosing between good and evil works:

> Understand, my children, that two spirits attend to a person, the spirit of truth and the spirit of deceit. Between these is the spirit of the intelligent mind, that inclines us however it wills. (*Testament of Judah* 20:1–2)

On the one side, we have God's spirits, and on the other side Satan's spirits. Between these two, we have another spirit: the mind. This is the one spirit to rule all the others. We use the mind spirit to think and make choices.

In the end this mind spirit is the ultimate weapon against sin. We can use it to overrule the evil impulses and choose good. Or, as we have free will, to overrule good impulses and choose evil—that's a bad idea though.

HERMAS CHOOSES BETWEEN THE SPIRITS

Everyone must use their "mind spirit" to choose between the spirits. This is a complicated undertaking, so many authors spend many words on this topic. One of these authors wrote the *Shepherd of Hermas*, and this is a fun place to read about choosing between spirits.

Hermas is a Christian book written around thirty years after Revelation. It's about a liberated slave named Hermas, who is now an elder of the Roman church. The book tells us how an angel came to visit him, and shared all manner of information with him. Hermas writes down five visions, twelve commandments, and ten parables. As we discussed earlier in the chapter on how the canon came to be, *Hermas* was almost included in the New Testament.

The sixth commandment, or sixth mandate, is a great place to visit on our journey of discovery. This commandment tells how you can know what you are meant to do:

> "I commanded you," he said, "in the first commandment to keep faith, fear, and restraint."
>
> "Yes, sir," I said.
>
> "But now," he said, "I want to show you their power, so you can understand something of their power and how they work. They work in two ways: the right way and the wrong way. You, trust in the right way and do not trust in the wrong way. The right way has a straight path, but the wrong way a crooked path. But you, walk on the straight and smooth path and leave the crooked path alone. The crooked path has no thoroughfare, but only rough ground and many obstacles, and is jagged and thorny, dangerous to travelers on it. But those who go the right way walk smoothly and without obstacle; it is neither jagged nor thorny. So you see that it is better to go this way."
>
> "It is a pleasure, sir," I said, "to go this way."

"Go ahead," he said, "and whoever turns to the Lord with a whole heart will go this way."[2] (*Shepherd of Hermas* 35:1–5)

Hermas tells us of the two roads that a person can follow in his life. There is a beautiful, flat, and tempting road, and there is a winding, dangerous one. That's an image that you might have heard before, but usually told the other way around. *Hermas* wants you on the easy road, and far away from the hard one.

Two Roads

I think that the first time the correct road is portrayed as a difficult path is from a book written in 1678. *Pilgrim's Progress* tells the story of a man who is on the way from the City of Destruction to the Celestial City. On the way he must, as every traveler must, choose between roads. It is abundantly clear that the most difficult road is the best one. Why? Because as we compare the two roads to life, it's most difficult to keep doing good.

While 1678 seems very long ago, the idea of following the difficult road is a new one for Christianity. More than 1500 years earlier *Hermas* wrote about two roads, and advised following the easiest one. Why? Because the easiest road takes the shortest route to God. If you choose the difficult path, you might get lost or waylaid, and then you really are in trouble.

The difference is in how you imagine the path. What do the difficulties on the path represent? In *Pilgrim's Progress* the difficulties are keeping the truth, living a good life, holding fast to the commandments. Those are difficult things, but it is good to uphold them. *Hermas*, on the other hand, sees the difficulties as sin. Sins are hard, because they keep you from God. Just as a winding road with many thorns would. So, we should stay away from sin. *Hermas* and *Pilgrim's Progress* ultimately say almost the same thing, but place different emphases leading to a totally different use of the same metaphor.

One Angel per Road

So, in *Hermas* we see faith, fear, and self-control as two paths. The easy, flat path is the best one. The winding, dangerous path is the bad one. Now that we have that straight, we can dig a little deeper.

2. The quotes from the *Shepherd of Hermas* are from Osiek, *Commentary*.

7. Spirits

> "Now listen," he said, "about faith. There are two angels with a person, one that is right and one that is evil."
>
> "So how am I to know, sir," I said, "the workings of each, since both angels live with me?"
>
> "Listen," he said, "and you will understand them. The angel of right is sensitive to shame, meek and tranquil. When that angel enters your heart, it immediately speaks with you about justice, about purity, about reverence, about contentment, and about every right deed and every honorable virtue. When all of this enters your heart, you know that the right angel is with you. These are the works of the right angel. Believe in it and its works." (*Shepherd of Hermas* 36:1–3)

So, now this is clear. There are two angels near every person. It's almost the same as in cartoons: an angel on one shoulder and a devil on the other, both whispering in your ear. Back then people had a slightly different image: each person has two (groups of) spirits inside of their body. They didn't see any difference between an angel and a spirit. The good spirits give you good desires, the evil spirits evil ones.

In this way these spirits can enter your heart. People then saw your heart as the most important organ. Not because it pumps your blood around, they hadn't figured that out yet. It was the most important organ because you use it to think. Every heartbeat is a thought. So a spirit entering your heart, is a spirit entering your thoughts, entering your mind. In other words, *Hermas* describes how a good or evil spirit can take over your mind spirit.

If you have an almost inexplicable urge to do good, then the good spirit has entered your heart. We need to keep on our toes and keep using our mind spirit to differentiate between good and evil spirits. Because, if you use your mind-spirit well and you notice that there is purity in your heart, then you have the good spirit. Listen carefully to him.

The Evil Angel

Besides the good spirit, there is also an evil angel. How do you recognize the evil angel? That's not very difficult.

> "Now look at the works of the angel of evil. First of all, it is bad-tempered, and bitter and stupid, and its works are evil, undermining the servants of God. When this one enters your heart, know it from its works."

> "How am I to recognize it, sir?" I said, "I do not understand."
> "Listen," he said. "When bad temper or bitterness overcomes you, you know it is in you; then come desire for doing more business, for extravagant food and drink, reveling, varied and unnecessary delicacies, lust for women, avarice, arrogance, pride, and whatever else goes along with them. So when these things enter your heart, you know that the angel of evil is in you. So when you recognize its deeds, stay away from it and do not trust it at all, because its works are evil and inappropriate for the servants of God. Now you have the workings of both angels; understand them and trust in the angel of right." (*Shepherd of Hermas* 36:4–6a)

Hermas has lost the plot, but we can keep up. If you suddenly have a strong need for an extravagant lifestyle, you have caught the evil angel. I often tease my wife with this. Her biggest temptation in life is over-the-top food. So, as we walk through the market she'll see stuffed mozzarella with lamb ears and arugula (or something equally ludicrous) and then she just has to try it. I always remind her: "Oh, no. You've caught the evil spirit." I am the first to admit that my theological knowledge does not always help my marriage.

But back on track, in Hermas's eyes waste, wealth, and luxury were bad. That's quite understandable coming from an ex-slave. He'd seen his share of all three and clearly understood that they don't come from God. You can recognize the evil spirit when you desire unnecessary luxury, when you are arrogant, and when you are greedy.

Watch Out!

Your mind spirit must keep its eyes peeled. As soon as it notices these things coming to mind, you must not listen. It is the evil spirit talking. Furthermore, you need to do anything you can to make sure the evil spirit has no space:

> Now you have the workings of both angels; understand them and trust in the angel of right. But keep your distance from the angel of evil, because its teaching is evil in every action. Even though a man be completely faithful, if the thinking of that angel enters his heart, that man or woman is bound to sin somehow. And again, even though a man or woman be really evil, and the work of the right angel enters their heart, he or she will necessarily do some good. (*Shepherd of Hermas* 36:6b–8)

7. Spirits

Apparently there comes a time when it is no longer a choice. If one of the spirits gains the upper hand, then the mind spirit will automatically do what that spirit suggests. If the good spirit gets enough space in your heart, you will do good deeds—even if you are a terrible person. The same with the evil spirit, except then you will sin, no matter how good a person you are.

So, you really should not let it get that bad. Recognize the actions of the evil spirit in time. Avoid those deeds and make sure that your mind is free of the evil one. Do not, whatever you do, let the evil spirit get so much space that you sin without thinking. That would be a disaster.

BACK TO JOHN

As we return to our path, we recognize Hermas's discussion with the angel in 1 John. Do you remember that we thought John's worries to be a bit strange? We concluded that testing demons that inhabit you would be rather easy and pointless.

Returning to 1 John, we arrive at a paragraph that is meant to be a light snack. 1 John was a fun structure, strangely similar to this book. The book contains interesting, lighthearted parts that are punctuated with short, very informative, and much deeper parts. First John 4:1–6 is one of those theoretical, deep-delving parts, and that is exactly the bit we are interested in. It is not directly connected to the previous section, and stands pretty much alone.

The passage discusses testing and differentiating between spirits. Something that, at first glance, is not terribly complicated. But with the *Testament of Reuben* and the *Shepherd of Hermas* in the back of our minds, this is an entirely different story. Spirits do much more than make you blind, deaf, or dumb. This passage in 1 John is suddenly much, much clearer. It is very much the same as we read in *Hermas*, just a lot less detailed:

> Beloved, do not believe every spirit, but test the spirits to see whether they are from God; for many false prophets have gone out into the world. By this you know the Spirit of God: every spirit that confesses that Jesus Christ has come in the flesh is from God, and every spirit that does not confess Jesus is not from God. And this is the spirit of the antichrist, of which you have heard that it is coming; and now it is already in the world. Little children, you are from God, and have conquered them; for the one who is in you is

greater than the one who is in the world. They are from the world; therefore what they say is from the world, and the world listens to them. We are from God. Whoever knows God listens to us, and whoever is not from God does not listen to us. From this we know the spirit of truth and the spirit of error. (1 John 4:1–6)

John tells these Christians that they cannot simply trust all spirits. Not every spirit is a Spirit (with a capital S) . . . there are many, many spirits. Only a certain amount of them come from God. Just as we saw in the *Testament of Reuben* and the *Shepherd of Hermas*: each human is under the influence of a large number of spirits.

It's not always immediately clear if these spirits come from God. John links the spirits to prophecy and confession first, and then good and evil deeds. *Hermas* told us that you knew you had become influenced by an evil spirit if you did evil things or had evil impulses. John portrays this as inspiration. The spirits inspire you to good or evil. The link to inspiration is easy to make, just look at the Old Testament (Isaiah 61:1; Ezekiel 11:5). Or even easier, just consider that inspiration literally means in-*spirit*-ion.

If you have the good kind of inspiration, teaches John, that is if you confess that Jesus came as a human, then the good spirit is in control. But if a spirit whispers anything else in you, you are in deep trouble. That spirit has been sent by the anti-Christ. While for many contemporary Christians the antichrist is very much something associated with the end of days, early Christians saw his influence in the world around them. It's probably best to understand that his antichristian power works through the ages, just as Christ's power works through the ages.

The great opponent, the ruler of this world, inspires false prophets with his spirits. These people act like they are prophets, but are in fact not speaking on behalf of God. These people are truly inspired by a spirit, but sadly not by the Spirit of God. Christians have run into these false prophets for ages, and should keep resisting them.

As Christians, as citizens of God's new world, we must keep ourselves focused on his new world. The false prophets get their inspiration from this world, but Christians have a better source: the new and better world to come. Heavenly power is always stronger than earthly power.

Now, I know we just finally got back on the path. We are all tired from our detour, but I see something very exciting, just off the path. It's in *Hermas*, we were just there. I can't help myself, we have to go have a look.

7. Spirits

Heavenly and Earthly Things

> "But you, trust in the spirit that comes from God and has power. Do not trust for anything the spirit that is earthly and empty, because there is no power in it; it comes from the devil. Listen to the parable I am going to tell you. Take a stone, throw it up to the sky, and see if you can touch it. Or again, take a water pump and squirt it up to the sky and see if you can bore a hole in the sky."
>
> "Sir," I said, "how can these things be? Both things you have said are impossible."
>
> "Just as these are impossible," he said, "so is it impossible to empower feeble earthly spirits. Take hold of the power that comes from above. The hailstone is an insignificant kernel, but when it falls on someone's head, what pain it causes! Or again, take the drop that falls from the roof tile onto the ground and makes a hole in the stone. So you see that the littlest things from above that fall upon the earth have great power; just so, the divine spirit that comes from above is powerful. So trust in this spirit, but avoid the other one." (*Shepherd of Hermas* 43:17–21)

Hermas has clearly never heard of gravity. But that's not that strange, because Newton only posited that theory fifteen centuries later. Thanks to his ignorance, Hermas does have a wonderful metaphor. There are two types of spirits: earthly spirits and heavenly spirits. Earthly spirits are, naturally, from Satan, the ruler of this world. The heavenly spirits come from God, who lives high in the heavens. The earthly spirits are evil, but they are also impotent compared to the good, heavenly ones.

To try to explain why the heavenly spirits are much better and more powerful than the earthly ones, the angel uses two examples. The first is that of a hailstone. It's a small meaningless piece of ice, but you don't want to get it on your head. That hurts a lot more than you would expect! Why? Because it has, thanks to its speed, much more power than you would think.

The same with a drop of water. No one would call a drop of water powerful. But if the water drips from the roof, it will eventually make a hole in the rocks on the ground. All of this is because, explains the angel, they come from heaven. Heavenly things just simply have more power than earthly ones.

The angel's conclusion is correct, but you could wonder about his explanation. We only wonder, however, because we now understand gravity. These are two great comparisons and the lesson is clear.

Earthly Prophets

The metaphor from *Hermas* helps us to understand John even better. The false prophets have no power at all. They ground their inspiration, their power, in this world. Their lessons are about this world and their message has no power. They are only interesting for people who are used to the powerlessness of this world.

But the children of God, as true prophets, ground their power elsewhere. They come from God, from his new world. Their inspiration is truly powerful: the Spirit of God. Their message is about a new world, not about this temporary, impotent one.

The spirit of truth is the spirit that inspires this powerful message. The spirit of error, the evil spirit, inspires people to nothing and nothingness. Only by using your mind spirit can you distinguish between these two spirits, by looking at the message and the inspiration. Is it about Christ? Is it about the new world? Then it's good. Is it about this world and its things? Then it's the evil spirit.

This does not mean that you cannot speak of earthly things. Of course not. But the entire message should not be about this world, and the message cannot be grounded in this world. If it is, you have a problem. Now we know why we need to be able to distinguish between the spirits, and even better, how to do that.

ACTS ALSO HAS SPIRITS

I just can't resist, now that we are talking about spirits, to look at the Holy Spirit and Pentecost. We've been talking about spirits for a while, but the Spirit is a different kettle of fish.

In ancient times the words "angel" and "spirit" were almost synonymous. That is quite logical because we generally assume that the evil spirits of this earth were once angels. God's angels are often just called spirits and Satan's spirits are often called angels. For the early Christians it became clear that, of all the good spirits, one spirit was better than the rest. This special spirit was the Spirit that Jesus promised to his disciples.

"You will be baptized," promised Jesus, "with the Holy Spirit not many days from now . . . . You will receive power when the Holy Spirit has come upon you" (Acts 1:5–8). Apparently this spirit is not just a holy spirit, it is

7. Spirits

the Holy Spirit. This very special Spirit is part of the trinity, and thus part of God. The other spirits are simply in the employ of God.

Pentecost

During Pentecost, the disciples were hanging out together. Pentecost is the celebration of the ten commandments and the Torah. It is the celebration of Sinai. While the disciples were celebrating, a special Spirit came down upon them. That was no coincidence. The disciples were celebrating the covenant that the Lord had made with their people thousands of years ago, and at that precise moment the sign of the new covenant became visible: the disciples received the Holy Spirit.

> When the day of Pentecost had come, they were all together in one place. And suddenly from heaven there came a sound like the rush of a violent wind, and it filled the entire house where they were sitting. Divided tongues, as of fire, appeared among them, and a tongue rested on each of them. All of them were filled with the Holy Spirit and began to speak in other languages, as the Spirit gave them ability. (Acts 2:1–4)

Suddenly they heard from heaven a sound like a strong wind, and they saw something that looked like fire. If you read carefully you will see that Luke does not say there was any wind. He also does not say there was any fire. There was something that seemed like wind and looked like fire.

What Do Spirits Look Like?

Like wind and like fire is exactly how most people thought spirits looked. We have already seen that spirits were supposed to be air or wind. Spirits are in the air all around us, they are invisible, so they must be made of air. They are even called *pneuma*, which just means wind, air, or breath. But that spirits were made of fire is something we have not yet discussed.

Air has very little power, but spirits have a lot of power. So spirits cannot be made only of air. They must exist of something much more powerful: fire. Generally, ancient people believed spirits to be made of air and fire.

That is exactly the image that we read in Acts 2. A description that perfectly fits how people imagined spirits. There was something that was like a mighty wind and something like tongues of fire: it was a spirit! A huge spirit arrived, so something that sounded like lots of wind. That spirit distributed itself over the people present, so small parts of the spirit, that resembled fire, rested on each of the disciples.

When the spirit, the Holy Spirit, descended on the disciples he filled them. That is an important word. The spirit did not just enter them, it filled them. The Greek word (*pimplèmi*) means something along the lines of filling until nothing more can be added; not a single drop. You know how that works. You can fill a glass and the water stacks up and reaches above the top, but just does not overflow—that's *pimplèmi*. The disciples were so full of the Holy Spirit that you could not add a single drop of another spirit. No spirit would have any space to enter them.

Gifts of the Special Spirit

This Holy Spirit gave the disciples a very special gift during Pentecost. The spirit let them speak in the languages of other nations. Elsewhere we see that the Holy Spirit gives other gifts to the believers: prophecy, service, leadership, wisdom, encouragement, and many others.

The people of that time imagined this as if a new, different spirit lived inside of them. Just like the other spirits that they already had, the Spirit of God lived in a specific organ. Which organ that was, becomes clear from the letters of Paul. He tells the Corinthians that the Spirit is in our hearts as a first installment or deposit (2 Corinthians 1:22). That special Spirit, that is part of the triune God, sits in your heart, closest to your thoughts. In the exact same place as your mind spirit, so that the Holy Spirit can help you make decisions.

SPIRITS IN A NUTSHELL

Sadly, every chapter must end, and so must this one. We only had time to look at two places in the New Testament where we run into spirits, but there are so many more.

Jesus says in John 4 that we must worship in spirit and truth—an intriguing thought. Simon the Magician is so impressed by the Holy Spirit that he wants to buy it from Peter. Jesus tells us how spirits roam the earth looking for people to inhabit in Matthew 12.

But now, after this chapter, you have, what we'd nowadays call, off-road experience. You can study those passages on your own, and see what your

7. Spirits

extrabiblical knowledge adds to your understanding of those parts of the Bible. On this walk we took two turns straight into the wilderness, but now we are back on the road. We have returned home safely, ready for our next walk. You will have to take that walk by yourself, without me to guide you.

H. Quite the Trip

Walking with my brother is always a bad idea. More accurately, it is the best worst idea that you will ever have. Adventure awaits you, as do new experiences. But so does exhaustion, fear, and danger. At the end it is all worth it, but on the way it's quite the challenge. Walking with my brother Paul means always taking the most exciting route—finding every challenge you can. It means doing things in the most difficult way possible.

We are done with our "Paul" walks in the Bible now, after seven adventurous journeys. We walked to the heavens, and past Satan. We took two trips around the Messiah, and we hiked to the hereafter. We even met Melchizedek on the way. On our last outing, we strolled past the spirits. Along the way we had new experiences, gathered more information, and came to a deeper understanding of the Bible. We heard some strange stories, we explored some deep caves, and we read about impossible physics. Each time we returned home, strengthened and secure. After taking a quick break, we were ready to set out again on a new walk.

Sadly, this book is now finished. We had seven extreme walks planned, and all seven are now over. If you stayed with me for the whole trip, it's likely you will never be able to look at the New Testament in the same way again. I have enjoyed these journeys with you—I hope you enjoyed them too!

Bibliography

Andersen, F. I. "2 (Slavonic Apocalypse of) Enoch: A New Translation and Introduction." In *The Old Testament Pseudepigrapha: Vol. 1 Apocalyptic Literature and Testaments*, edited by James H. Charlesworth, 91–221. London: Darton, Longman & Todd, 1983.

Brannan, Rick, et al., eds. *The Lexham English Septuagint*. Bellingham, WA: Lexham, 2012.

Bruin, Tom de. *The Great Controversy: The Individual's Struggle between Good and Evil in the Testaments of the Twelve Patriarchs and in Their Jewish and Christian Contexts.* Novum Testamentum et Orbis Antiquus 106. Göttingen: Vandenhoeck & Ruprecht, 2015.

García Martínez, Florentino, and Eibert J. C. Tigchelaar. *The Dead Sea Scrolls Study Edition*. Leiden: Brill, 1997.

Isaac, E. "1 (Ethiopic Apocalypse of) Enoch: A New Translation and Introduction." In *The Old Testament Pseudepigrapha: Vol. 1 Apocalyptic Literature and Testaments*, edited by James H. Charlesworth, 5–89. London: Darton, Longman & Todd, 1983.

Jonge, Marinus de. "The Testaments of the Twelve Patriarchs." In *The Apocryphal Old Testament*, edited by Hedley F. D. Sparks, 505–601. Oxford: Clarendon, 1984.

Nickelsburg, George W. E. *1 Enoch 1: A Commentary on the Book of 1 Enoch, Chapters 1–36; 81–108*. Hermeneia: A Critical and Historical Commentary on the Bible. Minneapolis: Fortress, 2001.

Osiek, Carolyn. *Shepherd of Hermas: A Commentary on the Shepherd of Hermas*. Hermeneia: A Critical and Historical Commentary on the Bible. Minneapolis: Fortress, 1999.

Verrecchia, Jean-Claude. *God of No Fixed Address: From Altars to Sanctuaries, Temples to Houses*. Eugene, OR: Wipf & Stock, 2015.

Wintermute, O. S. "Jubilees: A New Translation and Introduction." In *The Old Testament Pseudepigrapha: Vol. 2, Expansions of the "Old Testament" and Legends, Wisdom, and Philosophical Literature, Prayers, Psalms and Odes, Fragments of Lost Judeo-Hellenistic Works*, edited by James H. Charlesworth, 35–142. London: Darton, Longman & Todd, 1985.

More Extreme Walking

If you want to read more extensively in extrabiblical books, there are some collections that you can look at. These seven are widely available and a good place to start.

Charlesworth, James H., ed. *The Old Testament Pseudepigrapha: Volume 1, Apocalyptic Literature and Testaments*. London: Darton, Longman & Todd, 1983.

———. *The Old Testament Pseudepigrapha: Volume 2, Expansions of the "Old Testament" and Legends, Wisdom, and Philosophical Literature, Prayers, Psalms and Odes, Fragments of Lost Judeo-Hellenistic Works*. London: Darton, Longman & Todd, 1985.

Ehrman, Bart D. *The Apostolic Fathers I*. Edited by Jeffrey Henderson. Loeb Classical Library 24. Cambridge, MA: Harvard University Press, 2003.

———. *The Apostolic Fathers II*. Edited by Jeffrey Henderson. Loeb Classical Library 25. Cambridge, MA: Harvard University Press, 2003.

Elliot, J. K. *The Apocryphal New Testament: A Collection of Apocryphal Christian Literature in an English Translation*. Oxford: Clarendon, 1993.

García Martínez, Florentino, and Eibert J. C. Tigchelaar. *The Dead Sea Scrolls Study Edition*. Leiden: Brill, 1997.

Sparks, Hedley F. D., ed. *The Apocryphal Old Testament*. Oxford: Clarendon, 1984.

www.ingramcontent.com/pod-product-compliance
Lightning Source LLC
Chambersburg PA
CBHW031502160426
43195CB00010BB/1080